A [illegible]
A [illegible]

Over 15 years I sometimes imagined throwing the rings at him and walking away. Ultimately, they've been off my hand only three times, for cleaning. These rings have caught on my stockings, pulled on my sweaters, attached to stray threads as I glanced by. But they are a part of me.

Taking Off The Rings

"Do you know how to fish?" a skeptical Samantha asks.

"Sure, nothing to it," I say. Fearlessly, I stab another anchovy in the guts and head, thinking sadly of Caesar salad, then watch with sinking heart as the bait falls off the hook as soon as it hits the water.

"Can you help my Mom?" Samantha asks a guy whose arm says "Rosie, Kathy, Iris and Fran." "She's not doing so well."

Fishing Expedition

"Hi!" I say, and as I walk toward him he ever so furtively checks his watch. Twenty minutes later this is what we have between us: two drained coffee cups and a small arugala salad. The fork hasn't had time to defrost when he shakes his head.

"I'm sorry," Mike says sadly. 'There's just no magic here. I know magic when I see it. This isn't magic."

Give Me a Minute

"You're not insulted?" my mother had asked, when they bought their condo in Delray. Some people move to be with the grandchildren.

I told her then what she had told me when I first moved out to L.A. "Whatever makes you happy."

Queen for a Day

Also by Marlene Adler Marks

Nice Jewish Girls: Growing Up in America

The Suing of America: How and Why We Take Each Other to Court

A Woman's Voice

Reflections on Love, Death, Faith, Food & Family Life

MARLENE ADLER MARKS

11/6/00
JANA -
Here's to my decorating agenda
Thanks for being part of it

ON THE WAY PRESS • MALIBU, CALIFORNIA

Marlene

Library of Congress Catalog Card Number: 98-92267
A WOMAN'S VOICE: REFLECTIONS ON LOVE, DEATH, FAITH FOOD & FAMILY LIFE/Marlene Adler Marks

ISBN 0-9666432-0-8

First Edition
Printed in the United States of America

Permission to reprint Joan Nathan's recipe for "Tsimmes" on page 160 granted by the author.

BOOKS ARE AVAILABLE AT QUANTITY DISCOUNTS WHEN USED TO PROMOTE PRODUCTS OR SERVICES. FOR INFORMATION PLEASE CONTACT:
Published by ON THE WAY PRESS,
23852 Pacific Coast Highway, Suite 504, Malibu, Ca. 90265

For Samantha
To help you know what it was all about

ACKNOWLEDGEMENTS

A successful newspaper column depends upon a supportive editor and an equally supportive reading community. Gene Lichtenstein, editor in chief of *The Jewish Journal of Greater Los Angeles*, first encouraged me to write a personal voice column. For his on-going professional support, I am profoundly grateful. I am also thankful for the assistance of copy editors Stig Jantz and William Yelles and my dear friend and colleague Sara Eve Roseman.

The readers of *The Jewish Journal* have responded to my work with an immediacy and intimacy that I still find startling and wondrous. For this readership, I consider myself blessed.

Many of my friends saw our conversations reconstructed on these pages. For their support, I thank my great group: Cynthia Cohen, Olivia Cohen-Cutler, Joyce Fox, Jane Gassner, Barbara Goldberg, Marika Gordon, Willie Linsk, Susan Norman and Karen York who took these stories personally, and Leslie Wintner, friend and gifted graphic artist.

Finally, thank you, love and much more goes to my parents, Jack and Anne Adler, who saved every word of value I ever wrote.

Contents

PART TWO:
Family and Faith

PART THREE:
Food for Thought

PART FOUR:
More than a Single Life

Introduction: After Ten Years

A few weeks ago, I saw my husband walking across the street, near the dry cleaners. He was wearing khakis, a beige shirt and the brown belt I bought him for his forty-eighth birthday, the one with the gold buckle. I couldn't see the buckle, because I only saw him from behind. But I knew that it was the one I'd bought to match a new pair of shoes — a reddish, rawhide brown. I admired him from a distance: his U-shaped receded hair-line, his sturdy, wide neck, his fast-paced gait (acquired from the study of fencing and ballroom dancing.) He was amazingly graceful for a heavyset man. It didn't make a bit of difference that he's been dead 10 years.

I sped up the car to catch him, lowering my window so that I could say hello. The instinct to call out his name seemed completely natural.

As I was preparing to speak, I felt my face go flush and my mouth go dry.

"While you're at the market, we need some milk," I started to say.

"Oh, my God," I thought, "how do I explain myself now?"

You have to take my word for it: I do not live in the past. I do not go around expecting to see my husband on the Third Street Promenade or in the local market. I haven't dreamed about him since the second month after he died. He was riding his bike in a park, wearing a red-plaid shirt. He seemed just fine.

So, to see him now, to gasp in recognition, at a man with a similar body type and round head, was a surprising sign that, as with any amputation, the senses do survive.

The guy who could have been my husband's twin turned toward me. His face was stiff, and his eyes were dull, communicating none of Burton's understanding that life is a huge cosmic joke. I laughed. Then I imagined taking the stranger home with me, wondering what it would be like sharing even the kitchen with a man who appeared so much like the one I had loved, but who seemed to lack the salt of his cynicism and the pepper of his wit. Maybe the difference between the dead and the living is only a matter of taste.

But what if my husband, indeed, moved back in with us today, picking up precisely where we left off. What would he make of me now?

Take the house, for example. I couldn't bear to show him the back porch, with the outdoor sink sitting in a cabinet of corroded wood. And the living room, with the familiar chintz couch, its covers now worn thin. He'd sit down at the piano and immediately hear how badly it needs tuning. I mean to get to it, believe me, I do.

But it isn't only my neglect I fear showing him; it is that which I have done. Surely, he'd prefer the new white refrigerator over the avocado-green, and the low-pile white carpet over the sickening orange shag. And he'd understand that a child outgrows the wallpaper drawings of cows and geese and replaces it with photos of girls and boys her father has never met.

I've made an office of the garage without consulting him. I've gotten rid of most of the lousy paintings that were on our living-room walls. When he goes to unpack (I assume, for no good reason, that he has luggage with him), he'll find that the old bed and the bedspread have been replaced. And if he'd ask me what happened to our wedding photo, once prominent on the bedroom wall, I'd have to say, "I don't know."

INTRODUCTION

The phone would ring; a man would be calling. Maybe even several men. No use denying the obvious: I have known others. That must be why my face turned red.

I'd recognize him, but my husband might not recognize me.

The truth is, I don't recognize me either. I am a journalist by profession. I've spent more than 25 years covering law, politics and community issues. Yet what is gathered here is a strange kind of journalism indeed. These pieces, culled from nearly 600 articles written under deadline pressure week after week over the past 12 years, were largely written in the aftermath of my husband's death. They chronicle the inner war zone that is a family in mourning, and then the cease fire as the grieving stops and life resumes.

In the first years of writing my weekly newspaper column, I used to tell friends that my work was to open my vein and bleed on the page. Strangers, recognizing me from my tiny thumbnail newspaper photo, approached me in the market or in a restaurant, to ask, in worried tones, if I was OK and how my daughter, Samantha, then five, was getting on.

Those inquiries first unnerved, then strengthened me. The column became my lifeline to the world.

Why write a newspaper column from the midst of tragedy? Writing a personal column had been my dream from the beginning, though I took a while getting there.

I started out as the typical tough-talking, hard-bitten journalist, covering the courthouse for several daily newspapers. In the journalistic pecking order, my courthouse perch placed me half a step above police beat, which I would have enjoyed even more than the law, if truth be known. I loved action; I loved power. I loved dictating five new leads for my stories each day for the old *Los Angeles Herald-Examiner,* a real life Brenda Starr, thrilled to be on-the-spot about trials both big-time and obscure. Trials were civilized war. I felt I had entered the kingdom of heaven.

Newspapers are a very big deal in my family. My parents still read three or more papers a day. In fact, during my teenage years, when we weren't speaking to each other, my parents solely communicated with me by means of the daily newspaper columnists whose writings they clipped from the old *New York Post* or *Newsday* or *The New York Times.*

They placed the columns on my blue leather jewelry box before breakfast or after dinner. Mom left me the daily missives of Dorothy Schiff or James Wechsler or Max Lerner; Dad neatly cut out the Q&A format used by Dear Abby and Ann Landers and Dr. Joyce Brothers. From these writers warm observations and every-day insights, my parents found reassurance that our family was really OK.

That was the kind of writer I wanted to be: a member of the family.

My own early favorite journalists, Pete Hamill and Jack Newfield in the New York *Village Voice*, were more than reporters, they were the intimate voice of the city. Their writing said, we live here together and we're committed to each other. Nora Ephron in *Esquire*, Anna Quindlen in *The New York Times* and Ellen Goodman in the *Boston Globe* made clear the connection between politics and heart at home. Their beat was real life, and I was hooked on it. I hoped to become one of them. I wanted someone to pick up the newspaper and turn to me as a letter from a good friend. I never expected to open up so wide, and dig so deep.

"A Woman's Voice," is the name I took for my column in The *Jewish Journal of Greater Los Angeles*. It is the Hebrew translation of *kol isha*, the voice that so distracts men that they are forbidden to hear women sing during prayers. In the '80s, *kol isha* were fighting words, a political statement that many women took to represent the hurdles to be overcome as they set about reclaiming their Jewish lives. You will find here the personal columns that I wrote during the last decade, but much else was going on that my column also recorded. I have been part of that vast rediscovery, that joyous rebirth as women claim a heritage and an education barred to them for more than 1,000 years.

My first intention was to write about the changes that feminism was bringing to the world in which I lived, to write about spiritual and communal issues from a woman's point of view. "A splinter in the eye" is how one Talmudist referred to an educated daughter and I liked letting that Talmudist have a piece of my mind. Today, those educated daughters have forged a renaissance that has restored vibrancy to Judaism, and will bring an ancient tradition into the 21st century. I have reserved for another day my political columns, along with the great moments of history I've witnessed in Israel, world Jewry and in the American Jewish community, but rest assured they are there.

Within months of starting my column, my husband became sick. That's when I found my true woman's voice.

Burt and I had gone to Milwaukee for his bypass surgery scheduled on February 14, Valentine's Day. I was angry and scared. Burt had made the decision to go because the opposite was slow disintegration. "I'm a betting man," he said. As they wheeled Burt away, anxiety filled my throat and I could scarcely breathe. I feared not so much that I would faint as that I would be incoherent in the event anything happened to my husband.

So I did what has worked for me since childhood: I began to observe. This is not passive; it involves the focused engagement of eyes, mind, heart and breath. In the waiting room, I carefully studied whatever I could focus upon: the wallpaper, the TV set, the people huddled together on couches. I tried to make my eyes come alive, as if I'd never seen fern wallpaper before. I moved my eyes from "inside" my being, where I could only see that the surgery was starting so late that surely the surgeon would be tired, to the outer world around me. I took notes on the lined steno notepad I always carry with me. This insured that my eyes could not stare aimlessly into space but instead were compelled to fix on the page.

In the act of noticing, I grew still. How fascinating everyone in a hospital becomes, so long as they are not operating on *me*.

But what if they are indeed working on me? That's when the act of noticing became high stakes. In fact, right now, it is happening again, a man is approaching — the rabbi of our first story, "An Unwanted Visitor." He is coming forward with that awful professional smile. So now I'm operating on two levels, the me that is terrified, and the professional journalist who is watching a story unfold.

What a relief to be divided in two! I am panicked but I am observing my panic. By keeping one part of myself in the professional mode of observer, I can breathe again.

By the time Burt's surgery began, I had restored myself to a semblance of the extra-consciousness, the hyper-wakefulness that would serve me so well in the critical hours, months and years to come. I had to get through this ordeal not only for myself, but for my child at home in Los Angeles and the whole family that was depending upon me to be sane.

I returned from the hospital that day and, sitting at a word processor in my friend Gilda's home office, wrote my column to deadline, then faxed it back to my newspaper in Los Angeles. This was a double achievement: First, I stayed connected to the normal world outside the Milwaukee hospital. Second, I had a form — 900 words to write — and a promise to keep, since the newspaper was leaving space for me in its next edition.

And that's how these columns began. In that hospital room and in all the years since, I've kept myself alive through working at my writer's trade. In dark times or bright, in the midst of a rotten blind date, or while making gefilte fish, I notice everything; and in the act of noticing I become the competent self I need to be, and by force of habit have become.

After the first column about the rabbi was published, Burt died. Since 1987, my column, especially those about dating and about raising my daughter Samantha, has been left on teenage jewelry boxes, and family refrigerators, and e-mailed to daughters-in-law and grandchildren. It's been read from the synagogue pulpit, and even on the radio. How fortunate I am that my parents did not talk to me.

I was amazed to find that through my writing, I was no longer merely an objective journalist. I became that rare fortunate being, a writer who readers feel they can call by first name. Somehow, my willingness to write about pain, and joy even after pain, opened up the heart of readers. Today it's not my grief they share, but my joy and confusion in raising a teenager in a crazy world, my frustrations and pleasures as a single woman, and my connection to my parents and family, changing with time. The reader has been through much with me: a funeral, the mourning period known as *shiva*, blind dates, food and holidays, and boyfriends, love of child, spiritual growth. They tell me they know me and my daughter as well as their own children.

Without my readers, heaven knows what would have happened to me.

This book is arranged chronologically but certain themes emerge.

Part I is the deep tunnel of death and grief within

which Samantha and I were living. for the first year.

Part II is the effort to reconstruct our family life; we return to my New York roots of my parents, friends and relatives while Samantha and I rebuild our relationship on new terms, a mother and daughter alone.

Part III chronicles the revival of appetite. After Burt died, I ate little but baked potato and broccoli. Now I was hungry, for food and company. The recipes in this section are social foods, those you make to be with others. Not coincidentally, Samantha and I were preparing for her bat mitzvah, the rite of passage.

Finally, in Part IV, life goes on. My parents have retired, Samantha goes to high school, and I love again, briefly but well.

"Do you think you've gotten over it?" Samantha asks. My daughter knows all about counting time. On the anniversary of Burt's tenth *yahrzeit*, the memorial day of his death, she decided, it was time to move on.

I had to move on, too, and that's when I began to put these columns together as a book. I never once went to the cemetery unless my daughter demanded it. I had never watched home videos — I did not light the *yahrzeit* candle, being afraid. I couldn't look at the past because I loved it so much; I could not bear that it was, truly, gone. Time to move on, indeed.

In all these years, I have met many men and women who have suffered loss. We never think we do it right. We should have remarried earlier, or later, or not at all. We should have kept the house, or sold the house, or taken in a tenant. We become control freaks over the small thing — missing papers, unreturned phone calls — because we have no power over the large.

But what we never say is that death has great appeal. We study it and study ourselves, wearing it down like softened leather. Soon enough, memory serves us well.

Better than real life.

Real life gets messy; memory stands still. Real life is strange and frightening; memory consoles — even its pain is familiar.

We are lying on the bed, watching a home video. "Are you sure?" Samantha asks. "I don't want to cause you pain."

I teach her the word "catharsis" and tell her it is time. I have the *yahrzeit* candle ready. At random, we select the video from Burton's 56th birthday party, the year before he died. Usually, at these events, he was the family historian, spending most of his film trying to focus the camera lens against the Spanish tiles on the ground.

But, now, our friend Leslie has the camera, and it's time for the cake. We're all assembled, the birthday boy, his children, all his cousins and friends dating back to high school. I'm wearing a dress Samantha calls my "nightgown," and I've just dropped the cake I made on the floor, in the garage that would soon be my office.

"Here's the cake," I call out, feeding him a piece of chocolate mess. He laughs and kisses me and Samantha. And, I note, as he's busy eating, my husband had no time to make a wish.

Malibu, California
1998

Part One
Love and Death

"The proper course to adopt
with (loved ones) is to push away
with the left hand and
draw them near with the right hand."

Talmudic Expression

"Say a blessing for the bad things
that happen, even as you offer
thanks for the good."

Talmudic Expression

The Unwanted Visitor

MILWAUKEE — At some time, but not today, I may be able to write about my husband Burton's coronary bypass surgery, a surgery which has brought us to, and keeps us here at St. Mary's Hospital. St. Mary's has become a world-renown heart center because of its cardiac surgeon, Dr. W. Dudley Johnson, known as the surgeon of difficult cases. Burton, though only 57, is a difficult case, having suffered from profuse atherosclerosis over the years. We have come here in hope that through a tortuous six to 10 hour procedure Dr. Johnson has designed, Burton can again have a full life.

But it's too soon to write about the surgery, or Dr. Johnson, or even Burton and me. Not while danger looms so large in my life.

Instead, let me talk about a small thing, a tiny almost non-event that happened before the surgery ever started and unnerved me no end.

It is 4:30 p.m., and I am in the hospital's second floor Intensive Care waiting room, along with Burton's daughter, Peggye and our friend Gilda, a Milwaukee local. The surgery had been scheduled for noon, but postponed repeatedly by other surgical emergencies until finally it is to begin in 30 minutes.

Right now, Burton, is being prepped before being wheeled to the Operating Room about 100 yards down the hall, where, for starters, he will be anesthetized, sliced through the sternum and his heart placed on a heart-lung machine; veins taken from his legs will replace clogged arteries in his heart, and an intensive cleanup of Burton's arterial system undertaken.

I am prepping, too, in a way, laying in for the siege, armed with books, magazines, and stiff upper lip. Moments ago I said good-bye to Burton, who warned me about a check that had to be cashed, and now all that lies numbly before me in this room crowded with similarly waiting families, each subsumed in their own eerie silence, are the silver gray ferns on the wallpaper, the black second hand of the clock on the eastern wall and the endless drown of the television set playing *The Dating Game*.

And then he walks in, the air around him crackling with professional concern. He is tall, earnest and hurried, and I don't have even to see his *yarmulke* to know who he is or who he is here for. He is Central Casting's idea of a rabbi, and I know why he is in such a rush. Before he introduces himself, I know he is heading for me. And I want to run away.

Days later, when the nightmare of what would finally be a 14-hour vigil has receded, I talk with Rabbi Steven Carr Reuben of Kehillat Israel back home in Pacific Palisades.

"Yes, it can be awful," Reuben says of hospital visits that are part of every rabbi's daily duties. "I walk into a hospital room, and you can see the fear in their eyes. I have to say, 'Hey, it's O.K. guys. It's only me. It's Steve."

But it isn't Steve here in Milwaukee, it's Milt, and I don't know him from beans. Is it that I don't know him, or that he came to me uninvited, or that he is a primal reminder of what I am trying to forget? All I know is that Milt's here to comfort me and yet I feel my heart harden to him; I pull away, averting his eyes, resenting his innocent banter.

"Johnson's the best," he says.

Doesn't he know, it's too late to pump me up with

confidence? Even as Milt speaks, the dolly is rolling Burton away. I look at the rabbi but see instead only a Rabbi, an abstraction, an abstraction named Death.

"I'm sure it will go well," he says. I look at him blankly until, finally, the rabbi walks away.

As a symbol, a man in a *yarmulke* or a turned-around collar travels deep. On the morning of surgery, a priest, uninvited, enters Burt's hospital room (this is St. Mary's after all.)

"I'm going to give you a blessing." the priest says. Burt sat bolt upright in his bed, his face locked in a glare, terrified that by some mistake he would receive his last rites. The priest issued a neutral plea for his safety, and Burt, swallowing hard, mumbled "thank you."

But five days after surgery, as Burt lies fitfully in Intensive Care, disoriented and barely hanging on, recognizing no one, not even me, Milt pays him a visit. He says little more than hello. Yet Burt, who has never so much as seen Milt, instinctively seems to know what's up, and jumps to a conclusion. It takes hours for nurses to restore his composure.

My friend Miriam tells me a story. When her son Ted was 2, he underwent heart surgery. Miriam and her husband Michael sat the vigil alone at the hospital, a day spent in silence.

At one point, Miriam's family rabbi appeared, insisting on sitting with them.

"Get him out of here," Michael cried to Miriam. "He's making this a death watch!"

What gives religious representatives, Catholic or Jew or whatever, the right to assume that I would need, accept or desire spiritual comfort from a stranger?

But are they strangers? Aren't they more like members of the family, with assumed rights of access especially in times of trouble?

"People come here alone," Milt tells me a few days later. I have calmed down now, and can let myself be grateful for his interest in my "case." He's not a rabbi at all, (and never claimed to be) but an unpaid volunteer who for six years has worked under rabbinic supervision, drawn by compassion and interest to make life a little easier for the many Jews who, like me, search for miracles in Milwaukee.

"They're usually old, alone, staying in a hotel, and it's their last resort," he says. "And they see me in my *kippah* and immediately they know there's one of us here. Frequently, just the sight of me is comforting."

It hadn't been comforting to me; I couldn't handle it. I saw Milt approaching and felt from some place beyond words that there is a time when even a rabbi or well intentioned member of the tribe can do no good at all.

March, 1987

The Ways of Love

We were married on the hottest Labor Day on record, at my parents' Long Island home. Thirteen years later, here's what I remember: my grandfather's face as I walk down the aisle; my icicle hands and feet; Burt's adoring look; my mother's face, all concern and fear; nearly fainting on my father in front of the *huppah*; the rabbi complaining of the heat.

I felt that day as I have since the first time I saw him, alluring, fascinating, cherished, worthy. But not pretty. Believing that Burton thought me pretty came later.

The summer after we got married, we attended a July 4 picnic and were introduced to Megan, a friend of a friend, who is a television reporter on a local network. We've all been playing softball. Megan is blonde, blue eyed, thin. I look at her and all I can see is what I'm not: Gatsby's Daisy, the in-crowd, the 400. The All-American WASP.

And now, am I imagining it? She's coming on to my husband. Yes, I'm sure of it. She's flirting like Katharine Hepburn in *The Philadelphia Story*.

This is ridiculous. I am a mature woman now, I've had successes of my own. And yet watching Megan, so intensely vivacious listening to Burt, I am hobbled with envy. My thoughts are appalling: she's after my husband because she finds Jewish men sexy; she'll steal him away from me while I go to the bathroom. I'm filled with anguish and self-loathing and the only thing that helps is that she has lousy skin.

"You like Megan! You let her flirt with you!" I scream

to Burt in the car after the fireworks.

"You're imagining things."

"I am not. You like her. You like her looks. You think she's pretty."

"I think you're pretty."

"Don't patronize me. I'm 'Jewish pretty.' It's not the same thing."

Will I ever believe him?

"Look," he sighs. "There's more to life than looks."

We met in court when I wrote about one of his cases. Accompanied by his entourage of assistant counsel and clients, he blew into the state courthouse carrying two heavy briefcases and the aura of Clarence Darrow. I was a year out of graduate school, wearing a mini-dress I'd sewn myself, and a cynicism beyond my years. Here was my match, riding a motorcycle to court, a huge, hulking guy in a black leather jacket.

He studied cooking and owned a restaurant in Beverly Hills, where he took me the night we met; Anne, the Cordon Bleu-trained chef, served us quail eggs. He sings in a barber shop quartet, was an angel in a Broadway play, produced a long-running musical in Los Angeles.

By the time I met him, Burt had argued five cases before the U.S. Supreme Court, defending the rights of drug dealers, pornographers, prostitutes and petty gamblers. He has no concept of evil. His unsavory clientele is a challenge; he studied acting, and knows how to make love to judge and jury, which helps explain why one of his big-time drug dealers stayed out of jail for 17 years. He gets paid in cash, or diamonds or minks, but usually less than he was worth.

He brought a briefcase full of legal work even here, to the Milwaukee hospital.

His mother, Mary, took me to dinner soon after we met to set me straight about her son.

"He's trouble. Don't you see what you're doing?" she

asked. Burt's father, Sam, had been 18 years her senior, the same difference between Burt and me. When Burt told my parents he intended to marry me, my mother stopped breathing. But Dad asked only one thing: give up the bike. And he did.

Burt doesn't believe in diet, or sacrifice or guilt. Religion and God are superstition. After his first heart attack, Burt checked himself out of the New York City hospital and walked back to our hotel. An empty Teutscher's bag, stained with chocolate, fell out of his raincoat pocket. My brother, Alan, who sat with me in the dingy waiting room, wanted to slug him.

I can't restrain him. He of the grand spirit, the dramatic gesture. He bought our house after 15 minutes because he loved its view of the ocean at sunset. He still dares to eat caffeinated coffee and eggs! Last spring, on Friday he had heart failure. The following Monday we flew, as planned, to Rome. We made love with the window open to the hotel fountain.

Sometimes, I lie in bed at night, listening to him breathe. Terror, trauma, generosity and great love, are wrapped all in one. From my pillow, I gaze across the hallway, where in a small bed our little girl sleeps in innocence.

Magic runs between us. The sound of his voice soothes; the touch of his skin, the fold of his upper arm, stabilizes me.

I pull myself up next to him, running my hand over his back, he wraps his leg around my foot. With this man, I feel my own beauty.

March, 1987

Special Pleading

MILWAUKEE — The temple is lodged in an old brick house in a wealthy part of town. I am a stranger in this city and I am needy, because my husband is critically ill. I am drawn here by an intense yet invisible force: It is Saturday and going to temple is what needy Jews do.

I walk through the heavy oak door into the sanctuary and am greeted by the shrill warble of a young boy chanting the *haftorah*, an excerpt from the Prophets: I feel at home.

But then I notice that I cannot see the boy, nor his father, nor the rabbi, nor the thirty or more men I sense are to the left of me. There is a rustling of bodies and I hear their voices, chanting along, kibbitzing among themselves. If I crane my neck I can see the curly black tops of masculine heads, but I cannot see even their faces because there is a *mechitzah*, a high wood wall taller than I am, dividing us.

Facing forward, I can barely discern the Torah ark (skewed toward the men's side) but I can't see any part of the wide wooden table on which the Torah is placed for reading, nor the lectern from which the rabbi delivers his sermon.

Now I see: I'm in an Orthodox synagogue (specifically, Lubavitcher). I am on the women's side.

It must be some kind of cosmic joke on me, the great feminist, to find myself by accident dependent here upon this enclave of entrenched ritual, the very kind I spend my normal life trying to change. It strikes me at first as obscene: The whole set-up, the architecture of the room and the way the holy furniture is placed bespeak a tradition in which I, as a woman, do not count. Catch 22. To be part of this spiritual community even for a morning, I must agree to act as if I'm not part of the human community. For the true community by this reckoning is men.

However, the fact is, it's lucky I found this shul at all, *mechitzah* or no, since the local Reform congregation has no daytime Shabbat services. I can just hear my critics at home laughing I told you so. This Orthodox congregation is just across the street from where I'm staying: Beggars, as they say, cannot be choosers.

Why have I come here? The answer surely is that I don't know what else to do. Rationally, all that can be done is being done and most of it cannot be done by me. I go to the hospital. I visit. In the bed, lying still beneath a white sheet, there is a man who is apparently conscious, but not much else. I talk to him. I squeeze his hand. "I love you," I whisper. "You'll be going home soon." Then I change the classical tape in the cassette recorder, and adjust the earphones, hoping that Beethoven will get through to him when I have gone.

I can't do anything! In the weeks before the surgery, we tried to imagine coming to a point like this. After all, the doctors had given him only a 20 percent success rate. So we had created a living will, and a legal document on his chart gave me power of attorney, to decide if his medical condition was irreversible.

"I won't be a vegetable!" he cried one night. But in the hospital, each nursing shift eyes the legal form anew, and they look at me as one who would kill her husband when he becomes inconvenient.

I feel clear-headed and slightly hysterical. I stand on my head or take long walks; anything to reverse the direction we are heading.

So here I am, with my open prayer book, standing

with the women. The ancient formula is what I want, the voodoo that can unlock the doors to survival. But I must believe in it, in these Hebrew words, and in the power of these strange men with long gray hairs and the costume of 19th century Poland on the other side of the divider. Together, I pray, our words will get through where alone I cannot.

What is prayer, especially during crisis, but the inchoate longing for power and deliverance. The eternal cry of "Help me!"

It is difficult to pray. I am easily distracted. The rabbi faces and addresses only the men during his sermon; I can't even see the Torah as it's being read, let alone go up to read from it myself. I feel a vague yearning to touch the Torah, but here, of course, that is impossible for me, a woman, to do. To get additional prayer books for our side, we women must ask young children to carry them from the men's side; we are forbidden there for even practical purposes. And after the brief sermon, literally all the women run out to tend the children.

The women leave, but I remain. I am not the first feminist to turn out of urgency to an old man in a gray beard. Barbara Myerhoff, the late anthropologist, turned to the Lubavitchers when she was dying of cancer. She cut her nails and went to the *mikvah* and prayed.

"A *me'shaberach,*" I say. "Please, I need a prayer for health," offering my husband's Hebrew name.

He turns away, approaches the Torah, and invokes the legal formula. I hear my husband's name. A kind of lunacy takes over, the lunacy of belief. It will make a difference, I say. In the midst of misery, the *mechitzah* and the blatant irritation of religious politics recede. I am praying for a miracle.

March 1987

Mourning

Burton died two weeks ago, and I'm learning how to mourn. After an eight-year battle with heart disease, his death is no surprise. But it is a shock. He had "recovered" briefly, coming home to be with Samantha and me. He even went back to work and pretended nothing had happened. But his heart muscle was badly weakened. He had repeated heart failure. We celebrated his birthday in the hospital, a final stay that lasted a month.

I mourn the whole man: fearless criminal trial lawyer, generous lover, loving father, terrible punster, great cook. He was 57. We'd been married 13 years.

Mourning him is not easy: Burton did not live in the past, did not look back even on yesterday, and he would not respect or value reverie in me. He'd tell me to clean out his clothes, close out his office — get on with life!

Still, death sticks my tracks. Certainly I've been grieving for years throughout his illness, but now I actually touch the unfathomable itself; like Emily in *Our Town*, I see the line separating the dead from the living and feel myself on the other side.

I gave the eulogy at my husband's funeral. Weird, right? I simply couldn't leave it to the rabbi, well-meaning though he would be, to offer the last lugubrious words. Am I play acting? At least acting is a choice, a pose which affirms an attitude. My attitude is that Burton Marks will not be mourned with tears of self pity, because he didn't live that way.

The role of wife, it seems, is not one I will easily relinquish. I will defend my husband even after death.

I know nothing about death, but I want something more from mourning than the predictable stages of Elizabeth Kubler-Ross. Kubler-Ross focuses on the dying, but I am, whatever it looks like, still alive.

The night Burton died, I was a lonely caravan of one driving from the hospital at 2:30 a.m., carrying the notebooks, the phone pads, brief case, and the shirts he wore — remnants of my husband's last days. Halfway home, I stopped at a pay phone and made a call.

"Rabbi, Burton's dead." I said. "Tell me what to do."

Three days of tears, seven days of lamentation, and 30 days to three months of neglect of the appearance, say our Sages about the rhythms and limits of mourning. The Jewish way never lets you linger in some eerily-indulgent psychological stage, but hooks me right back into the community where I long to be.

There are plenty of rituals for me to hold onto. The Jewish mourning calendar has a name for every phase.

Onen: In the first three days after death, I was one who has suffered a loss, and has no obligations other than making funeral arrangements. Members of my synagogue made all my meals and cared for Samantha.

Aninuth, the period of "outrage." I saw Burton, smelled him everywhere. The sight of his signature on a scrap of lined paper, the feel of his body's impression on the unused side of the bed, the warmth of his wool suits, each felt like an assault.

Shiva: The seven days of grieving after the funeral.

Shloshim: Thirty days of loss.

Kaddish: For 11 months (for the righteous, 12 for the wicked) I say the mourner's prayer, but then get back into normal life. Once the dead have been shown a respectful burial, it is the living who count.

Death is an education. My orientation has begun.

Baruch dayan emet. Blessed be the true judge.

June, 1987

Lesson In Community

For many years I've belonged to a professional and businesswomen's group under the auspices of a Jewish charitable organization. It's a networking group (!), and I had typical yuppie motivations for joining: the desire for professional and social connections, the possibility of political prestige or power. I eventually served on the board of this organization, and was speaker at several events. The women were nice and I thought we were friends.

In recent month, word got out that my husband was ill and then had finally died. Friends contacted me from all across the country; but from this group of comrades in my own town, nothing.

Not a call. Not a card. Not a word. I was crushed, but to be fair, I, too, never respond to births, illnesses or deaths among the members.

One day, during the illness, the phone rang. "I've been meaning to call you for months," said Phyllis, the group's former president. "But I've had troubles of my own. The reason I'm calling," she said, "is to ask you about your annual contribution. How much will you make it this year?"

I was stunned into silence. Two months later, Jeanie, another bigwig, called just after I completed *shiva*. She elliptically commented on my situation, then came to the point. "What will you do about your contribution?"

Now I was furious. Organizational silence to my plight seemed golden preferable to this heavy-handed alms-seeking. Such startling insensitivity might have been expected from stranger; from peers it left me reeling.

"Community" is a hot topic these days — everyone seems to agree there's a problem: that Americans are too individualistic, too narcissistic to create decent community life; we overcome these failures only from strong religious or ritual need. In general, however, it's the residue of The Lonely Cowboy; we can't commit to anything or anyone long enough to build relationships.

So perhaps my experience with recent widowhood can be helpful. The sad truth is that the whole social terrain changes in the face of a loved one's death, and community essentially collapses. In the last months, friendships have been crumbling all around me as I learn which of "our" friends were really Burton's and which will still be mine. I'm not taking any bets. People simply do not know how to deal with the survivors. No one is reliable, not even old and dear friends from way back when. There are no standards for friendship in times of stress, no way to hold people accountable. They don't know what to say in the face of the empty chair at the restaurant or the lost fourth hand at bridge.

It's silly to expect too much.The newly-grieving will find it easiest to live as if she has no one left, and then be surprised if any one turns up.

As for asking how you are, forget it. It is easiest just to skip over the difficult part of conversation and go right on to business. That's if they bother to call at all.

I can't hold these networking colleagues to the same standards of friendship, but even so, there's a certain hurt. And the confusion latent in these business situations will become increasingly widespread as women merge their social and professional lives. It may be hard to tell the difference between a professional friend and a real buddy. But death and emergencies will point it out clearly enough.

This only means that professional groups may soon have to behave like the old neighborhood volunteer organizations, and take an interest in the people who join, not merely their job slot. When my husband died, the bank, insurance company, even the car-leasing agency, all responded with sympathy and offers of personal accommodation. Yet the Jewish charitable agency we both nurtured with our dollars and time has yet to offer the first condolence. The computer continues to spit out dunning notices on my husband's donation account, and the women's network continues to harass me on mine. At the very least, charitable organizations should create committees to track the deaths of members, assuring that notes of sympathy are received by the deceased's family and followed up by phone.

I had joined that networking group looking not only for business contacts, but also friends. I believed that if I met young women with careers, and young families — women just like me — intimacy and commitment would naturally flow. It didn't happen.

Instead, I learned that sharing an abstract activity like fund-raising, even in the context of a worthy goal like helping the needy, does not insure that the gel of community will hold. Nor does sharing a common personal heritage or personal lifestyle. It's hard to say what will keep people together, in this era when it's every man or woman for herself and we're all so very busy. In the old days of neighbors and neighborhoods, a friend was one who would watch your child while you took a bath. In these days, friendship is all wet.

June, 1987

Kaddish

Let me say right off with respect to the mourner's Kaddish, I do everything wrong;

Nearly three months after Burton's death, I say Kaddish as the spirit moves me: after my morning meditation, while watching the sunset, at 3 a.m. when the bed seems too large.

I stand by our bedroom window looking out on the avocado tree: *"Yis-ga-dal v'yis'kadash sh'may ra-ba"* magnified and sanctified be the name of God — twenty-five seconds of the Aramaic intoned, as the tradition instructs, at a decibel level high enough to be acknowledged, but low enough not to wake the sleeping child in the next room. For during those twenty-five seconds, my husband comes to me: It is not much, hello and goodbye, but for a moment I grasp something — his eyes maybe or the feel of his skin — part of the aura which pervaded me while he was alive.

My mouth moves. A breeze comes through the window. I go on.

This is all incorrect. One does not say Kaddish alone: it is not a private prayer, its purpose (as opposed to its effect) is not to make you feel saner and steadier but to sanctify God.

The Talmud explicitly states that Kaddish is to be said as part of a community, that is, a minyan of 10 men.

That's my second mistake. I am not a man, and so have no legal obligation to say Kaddish at all. Once again, Kaddish is not said for therapy or personal indulgence, but for duty. The prayer does not mention death:

It initially began as a prayer of praise at the end of study sessions.

Now of course, Kaddish signifies honorable grief. To have someone say Kaddish for you is the very definition of immortality. That's why these days everyone at synagogue rises to say Kaddish for the Six Million, most of whom died leaving no survivors.

Why does the human spirit cling to ritual? In times of grief, it is so hard to think at all. We are thrown to the mast, terror at full gale. So ritual is the guidebook, a list of proven exercises, a way of saying "Here, do this. These words or actions worked for people just like you down through the ages. Give it a try. Can't hurt."

I remember the old men of my childhood synagogue rising to say Kaddish. What power and dignity they had, publicly declaring their loss. Maybe I should shlep into town for the daily minyan, but I won't leave Samantha.

So I say it alone. Nothing else but Kaddish gives vent to the inarticulate mixing of loss and perseverance that comprises my daily life. I don't understand a word I'm saying, yet this prayer says it all.

Since the 13th century, young men have stood during prayer service to say Kaddish for their fathers, honoring the deceased's memory and paying lip service to the ancient folklore that during the first 11 months the soul awaits judgment. I'm not sure I believe that Burton is awaiting anything, but parts of him are still hovering around, trying to make contact. I pray in solitude, in Hebrew known as "*tefillah b'yechidut.*"

Martin Buber calls religion a dialogue between I and Thou. Maybe God does not receive my calls. But as I stand with my prayer book before the avocado tree the breeze comes through the window. I go on.

Summer, 1987

Losing Daddy

"Why did Daddy die?" Samantha asks, whenever there is a lull, whenever she can find a reason. "When will he be alive again?"

"I'm sorry, he won't." I whisper.

"Is Daddy in heaven?"

"Who told you about heaven?"

"Jonathan."

"What else did Jonathan tell you?"

"He said God won't let little children die."

So Jonathan, a tow-haired Christian boy, has become Maimonides of the Schoolyard. He was just trying to comfort her. I do not do as well. I try to respond, but go numb.

We would have come to this point eventually, a talk with Samantha about death. Rocky, the preschool rabbit died a few months ago, and every parent was upset, facing the nightmares of three- and four-year-olds. But this of course is a different story. This is Daddy. Plus, I'm a mess myself and can barely find the words to explain anything.

Throughout the long dreadful last month, Samantha had been coming with me to the hospital. She became familiar with the elevator that stopped on floor 6, the nurses in the Cardiac Care Unit who brought her an extra vanilla pudding when Burton ate his dinner, and the unique wiring that monitored his heart. She would stare at the regular beating pattern, trying, I think, to figure out whether it was good or bad. He was tethered to three different devices, so it couldn't be good. But the nurses, the doctors and Burton himself remained cheery, so it couldn't be too bad.

She had grown to trust the nurses so well, that when he died she wanted to go back to the CCR, demanding to know what went wrong. We did go back one day, just to thank them, and she did her best to behave. But the recent weeks have been a living nightmare.

"The ambulance, Mommy. You drive the ambulance."

So we play: the ambulance pulls up, the paramedics get out. They wheel Burton out of the house and into the van. But this time in our imaginations something is different. Samantha gets to come along too.

"I'm going to make you better," Samantha says to Daddy. "You'll see, you'll be just fine."

But he isn't just fine. And the nurses did the best they could, which is hardly good enough.

"It's not fair. It's just not fair!"

Sometimes I rationalize that having faced death at such an early age, Samantha will somehow have it easier later, that ultimate issues will not prove so overwhelming to her. I know of course that this is nonsense, but it's the best I can do. It is completely, horribly unfair. She draws a family portrait: a tall mommy with a thin waist, a short daughter wearing a long dress. We both wear crowns. And we both have sharp teeth, almost fangs, hanging from our mouths. And our eyes stare out from huge spider-like lashes. "It's not fair!"

These ideas make me angry: that there is a heaven; that God is an old man with a white beard; that when our prayers for the Messiah are answered, the bodies of the dead will rise and walk on this earth. I never expect to see Burton again. I simply cannot even conjure up a place where such a meeting would be possible, not even under the cypress tree near where he is buried.

Still. There is a physical place, in the lower portion of

my heart where I hurt so badly, that the pain literally forces Burton to reappear. When I touch that spot, I can re-create from memory the smells, the texture of his hair, and his stupid punning joke. Then, as soon as I've conjured him into physical presence, I rail at him for leaving us with his paper work incomplete and with his life not nearly done. Memories are life ever lasting.

Samantha and I repeat our scenario again and again, making tracks in the soil of disappointed love. We visit the fire department and the paramedics who once saved his life. We play doctor, nurse and patient. We try new cures. Sometimes we even come home alive.

"Daddy loved me, didn't he?" she finally asks. Finally, when even Samantha finds this all intolerable, we read *The Trumpet of the Swan* and go on.

September, 1987

Seeking Mr. Right

My mother is subtle. The New Year's card she sent me called out "Gut Yuntif" and in her own hand she wished me a year filled with "exciting new beginnings." Hmmm. She doesn't mean a new book contract or a new client. A "new beginning" to the mother of a newly single daughter means one thing — new men.

"Anything interesting happening?" she asks in our phone calls. I tell her Samantha took the school bus to kindergarten by herself.

"That's nice. Anything interesting happening?"

You can't change the spots on a leopard. It's been 15 years since she's asked me that question, but what can you do? A mother is a mother, my mother says. And mine will not rest until I'm safely married again.

It's not just my mother who thinks about men for me. My friend Greg offered to pay for my personal ad in a local newspaper. Others say join a gym. The eagerness to see me back in the social swing is certainly not intended as disrespect for my late husband, nor does it indicate that they think I am nothing without a man. No, theirs is a simple message straight from an old Beatles tune: "Oh-bla-di Oh-bla-da, life goes on."

Life does go on. Five months after the funeral there are signs of time's haphazard passage all around. Lightbulbs burn out; a child grows taller; the indent in the right side of the bed disappears.

The question inevitably arises: When will I love again? Not whether but when. My mother and Greg say sooner rather that later, and for once I do not argue back.

On the subject of great love, the rabbis have this enigmatic expression: "Always let the left hand thrust away and right hand draw near." (Talmud tractate Sotah). They mean: Even as you are swept away by the love of another, even as you feel yourself completely one: Beware! Hold something of yourself in reserve. When you suffer loss, you must be able to go on.

There are days when memories of Burt cling like spiderwebs to every corner, every turn. It takes a mighty left hand to thrust them away.

They're so practical, these rabbis: They don't suggest finding a new husband is easy. "All things can be replaced, except the spouse of one's youth," (Sanhedrin, 22b). But, they say, if you've loved when you were young, you can love again, (Yevamot, 62b). I'm pinning their words to my mirror, for luck.

The next question is not the optimistic "when" but the sobering "who" the lucky man will be. Reading a score of singles ads, I can tell you it won't be any of the clone-like "SJMs" who purport themselves to be "45, professional, sincere, sensitive" and who "seek an attractive, slim woman for walks on the beach."

Are these guys for real? Here's the man I'm looking for: "SJM executive-type, well read and travelled, likes cooking, can fix a garbage disposal and use WD-40." Are my needs too great? I want a man who can use a sander! A man who knows his way into an electric socket! A man who can tell me why the Democrats should run Mario Cuomo!

The emphasis on the new "sensitive" male seems bizarre to someone emerging from the warm cave of a 13-year marriage. "Sensitive" to what? Do they all have acne or break out in hives when an unkind word is said? Whatever happened to traditional values of husbandry: the ability to make a good living, loyalty to home and family, and the desire to make a woman happy?

And who is this "attractive slim" woman they're seeking? "Attractive" to moths? To trouble? Are women to be weighed like cattle, by the pound? Tell me how long the "sensitive" male and his "attractive" mate will last when the wolf comes to the door.

The idea of dating new men makes me cranky and the latest Shere Hite report, *Women and Love,* merely exaggerates the condition. When 4,500 women were asked questions about their love life, "Are you happy with your relationship?" 84 percent said "no." According to Hite's survey, the double standard still exists despite the sexual revolution: 92 percent of single women report that men are in control of dating, still trying to "score" sexually with women whom they later dump.

So here it is, at the time in my life when I'm most realistic, open, free and independent, I'm facing not only the AIDS epidemic, but the age-old problem of male gamesmanship. Wake me when it's over.

(But, if the war between the sexes is so heated, women surely share responsibility as well. It takes two to tango, or used to. The Hite report nowhere indicates how women contribute to their own unhappiness, playing at being "submissive," attracted to men who use them, arguing from weakness. I'm no picnic, I can tell you.)

If I never date again, I'll be the happiest woman in Los Angeles. I don't like being a stranger, I don't like judging a man by his suit only to learn later that it's his only one. I even dislike the first five years of married life when all the things that attract you to a person become intolerable, and the qualities you may eventually admire have yet to emerge. But if I never marry again, well...

If I never marry again, I won't achieve the goal I never knew I had: growing old with someone I love. When I think of all the reasons why it would be worth going through the awkwardness of dating, the adjustments and misapprehension of the early years together, the inevitable mid-life crisis, health crisis or assorted financial and emotional reversals or disappointments, the only one that stands up is this: the prospect, really only a hope, that at the end of a very difficult road, we'd still be together.

Because from where I sit, that's the payoff. After the heat of youth dies off, companionship remains. It may be my imagination, but I see more of them now, older couples, surviving 30, 40, or 50 years together, exhibiting a kind of love which youth simply can't fathom.

It moves me so, to see them dance together, the touch of an aging male arm on a spotted female hand. And then I think of what I lost in Burt's passing, it is this most of all, the kindness between two people that only time together earns.

"Oh-bla-di, Oh-bla-da, life goes on." How life goes on.

September, 1987

The Expert

I used to fantasize about my life after Burton died. I would sit by myself, quietly, for weeks on end. That was all. Sit in quiet. Alone. Until Samantha came home from school, and then we would sit on the couch, and just cry.

This has not happened. I hate quiet. I like company. I cry when I have the need, but rarely on the couch. It scares Samantha to see me cry. To her, crying is a sign of broken heart, and a broken heart means heart surgery, which means I'll soon die. I cry anyway, of course, sometimes in the car, when I hear violins play.

I need a new kind of human companionship and find it, of all places, among my friends with whom I study Torah, the Hebrew Bible. Why here? Because in these continual meetings each Saturday I don't need to pretend that things are great, that I am continually competent, or that my stability has been restored. No one here bugs me, as some friends do, about how unruly Samantha can be. No one cares if I fall asleep rather than study. Remember this: the greatest gift you can give a person in crisis is the freedom to fall apart in front of you, without fearing judgment.

We've been reading Torah together for more than a year now, Harry, Rick, Brian, Ira and Jack and Gabby, and sometimes Robert, Ruth and Cheryl. Burt never came along, he thought studying Torah a form of fanaticism. Samantha and the other children play as we adults breakfast and kibbitz, and then diligently work our way, week by week, through the ancient text, moving from Genesis (*Bereshit*, in Hebrew, for the first word meaning "in the beginning,") and on through Deuteronomy, a full year.

The tragic stories in the Bible calm me. The worst that can happen to a man or woman is contained in that text. Cain kills Abel. Rachel dies in childbirth; Sarah, Rachel and Hannah live for years with infertility. Dinah and Tamar are raped, the first by the ruler of a town, the second by her father-in-law who mistakes her for a prostitute. Joseph is sold into slavery by his brothers. Sodom and Gomorrah are consumed by lust and greed, and destroyed in a holocaust. Ruth and Naomi are left penniless as widows and must feed off the gleanings of their relative Boaz's field. I find it all deeply reassuring, making my own problems seem small.

We are studying in some detail the world as an organic whole, from the Creation to the founding of the Jewish people, to the wanderings in the desert and on to the death of Moses. We trace the eternal cycle of birth and death as manifested in a year's living. When I was in Milwaukee, the Jews were just leaving Egypt. When Burt came home, they had received the Ten Commandments. When Burton died, Moses learned he wasn't going into Israel. We are moving together with the text, and we are not alone.

Only months after Burt died, another tragedy rips our group. Two weeks ago, Jonathan, Harry and Gabby's five-and-a-half month old son, slid under the rollbar of his stroller and choked. After hours in the UCLA pediatric emergency room, he died.

Hours before the accident, I sat with his father and others in the gerry-built hut called a sukkah reading Ecclesiastes while the little boy in the playsuit with sailboats practiced turning over in his playpen.

"What is crooked cannot be straightened, and what is missing cannot be counted," says Kohelet. Sun filtered through the palm-frond roof, casting autumn shadows.

I leave my own grief behind to be with them, trying as best I can to be an anchor in the whirlwind while others mourn. How does one behave in the face of senseless death? What use is there in pondering life's "meaning?" In searching for a moral? Know this, that the only thing to say at a time of tragedy is that it's all garbage, and the only thing to do is bring a casserole for the family to eat later in the week.

My friends all assume I'm a pro at this, that my heart has grown accustomed to suffering. I'm "the expert" on grief, or so they think. Yes, I've been through it before. I've made the arrangements. I've been to the mortuary. I've dealt with the rabbis. I sat by the gravesite. I've sat on low stools, and covered all the mirrors.

But I don't know anything. I don't know why horror happens, and I don't know how to console myself, let alone others, when the worst occurs.

I'm angry at God, whose power was significantly missing when Jonathan was in danger. But what good does anger do? Instead, I take care of practical details, calling the sisterhood president, planning for the memorial service, placing the table and a pitcher of water by the front door so those returning from the cemetery might wash away death and move into life. Later, I shovel dirt on the tiny coffin. I give hugs and I eat.

It is the most horrible moment, to watch helpless, a witness to grief, peering in from the outside. But this is what it means to be part of a community, to do what can be done, and to know that these will never feel like much. The wailing and the muffled sobs continue and my acts seem insignificant. But they need me here for the nightly prayer minyan. My presence gives these struggling people the freedom to fall apart, without fearing judgment. It is better to hear the crying together than to sit under the tree alone.

February, 1988

How A Single Mom Does Shabbat

When I was married, I made an elaborate Friday night meal: fresh challah, chicken or fish, and a special dessert.

I set the table early in the morning, and invited guests for the night. Before sitting down to eat, we stood at the table: a hush descended on us, as we lit candles, drank wine and broke bread. How civilized we were.

Now, er, hmm. I am a Single Mom and everything about being a Single Mom is different, including how a Single Mom does Shabbat, the crowning moment of the week.

Of all the family rituals that hold a Single Mom's life together there are two which are most prized: the nightly reading of the bedtime story, and the Sabbath family meal.

Whatever it does for my daughter, the bedtime story keeps me sane each evening, as Samantha and I mark our progress through *In the Night Kitchen* or my old favorite, *All of a Kind Family.*

But Friday night belongs to us in a separate way, a time dedicated not to fantasy stories but to reality, our reality, in our own home.

As a Single Mom, I have been sitting on the freeway for more than an hour by the time I get home from work on Friday evening. I am looking forward to a good meal. Throughout the week, naturally, I eat on the run; the regulation muffin-and-coffee breakfast, dinner from the take-out section at our local market, which I eat with a plastic fork directly from the container held on my lap as I drive home.

But Shabbat is different and it demands something which is eaten off a plate.

Pushing my way through the door, my arms loaded with groceries, I take off my shoes and kick them into the corner, dump the packages onto the kitchen counter, and preheat the toaster oven. I take four fish sticks out of the box in the freezer and dump them on a foil-lined metal toaster tray for broiling. I slice two carrots, toss them in a steamer and set the stove on to "high." So much for Friday dinner for Samantha.

As for me, I throw a baked potato in the microwave. In roughly 10 minutes, I'll mash the potato with Parmesan cheese. Add steamed broccoli — the plate needs color — and viola! Eat your heart out, Julia Child.

Running to the dining room table, I shove a week's worth of mail to the side. I take the store bought challah out of the bread box and set it on the silver platter, alongside the candle sticks and a wine cup. Samantha takes out the candles; having forgotten to buy wine, I pour Sundance cranberry drink into the silver goblet, hoping God will forgive me.

"Come on, Sam, let's do Shabbat," I call to my daughter now engaged in her 3,000th viewing of *Jaws*. Getting no response, I go after her and slam the tube off.

"O.K., kill the lights," I say. She hits the switch and we're in darkness. For a brief moment, Samantha and I look at each other, in thanksgiving for the week just passed. We say the prayers over the wine and bread and offer a quarter to our charity box for the poor; she eats her fish sticks in the living room watching *Jaws: the Avenger,* a rented videotape. I eat my baked potato in the dining room, setting my plate on a pile of bills.

By 8:30 we are both asleep.

Being a Single Mom has given me a new understanding of human fallibility. I have not yet bought whipped cream in an aerosol can, but I once picked it up longingly before buying the kind you beat from scratch. It's not that my standards are lowering, but here are some words I no longer use: "perfect," "correct," "spotless."

My mother used to tell me that the key to happiness is the ability to "look away," that is, the refusal to take seriously every dust ball under the couch, every dirty nail on a child's hand. Boy was she right: a Single Mom soon learns to love her blinders, she lives with the constant knowledge that the cat need its shots, the linoleum is peeling, and the checkbook remains unbalanced for the second year in a row, but how much can you do?

Oh well, Single Mom rests on the seventh day from her labors and says not that "This is perfect" but that "This is good enough."

All right, so I'll never get it perfect. Maybe accepting that fact is a relief. All around me, baby boomers with their new families are still aiming for perfection, the best stroller, the best kinder gym, starting their kids reading at six months. They long to create a "spiritually perfect" child, creative, perky, a Harvard MBA or a star in TV commercials, a child who won't rebel.

Once I was like them, somewhat smug, convinced that life is like a vast test kitchen in which the object is to get out all the kinks in the recipe. But I'm learning the hard way: There is no one recipe! There is no single right way! And if there is, *I'm doing the best I can!*

And anyway, gourmet education is bankrupt unless it teaches the basic, eternal values of hard work, kindness towards others, and respect for oneself.

I guess being a Single Mom has only made explicit what I've always guessed: Life's path is often lonely, but there is no alternative.

The children of Israel wandered 40 years in the desert, most of it in circles, gaining spiritual fulfillment.

Nothing happens overnight.

The point, if there is one, is to discover, in Leo Baeck's words, the holiness in everything, by which I suppose he meant even a dinner of fish sticks and microwaved potato. In our nightmares, our tragedies, we know God too.

Single Mom gets ripped off by the auto mechanic, sweet-talked by the electrician.

Taking out the garbage, I try to find the holiness here, but it's hard.

In the perfect Shabbat, each person blesses the other: the husband blesses his wife as a "Woman of Valor." The parents praise their children as worthy descendants of Abraham and Sarah.

Shabbat dinner over, Single Mom sits down by Samantha and nibbles on the little girl's carrot.

The killer shark has returned.

"I love you," I say.

The little girl nods.

"I love you, too, Mom."

One holy moment is good enough.

November, 1987

Dating Game

My first "blind date" was Melvin.

"Just say I'm in my 40's." he says on the phone. "I don't look my age."

We meet at a coffee shop. A doctor, harried, gray, balding.

"I'm making an exception for you," he says. "I never date women with children. But since your husband's dead I figure it will be O.K.."

I'm flattered.

"I want my own family," he says. "Ex-husbands are terrible. Ex-wives aren't too great either."

Next comes Harry. I know his father, a great guy.

"Don't ask me how old I am," he says on the phone. "I won't tell you."

"Let me guess. You're in your 40's."

"I don't think of myself as being in my 40's. I'll bet you can't guess how old my dad is?"

I guess.

"I won't tell you. If you know how old my dad is, you'll know how old I am."

That's how it's been going lately, life on the dating circuit. Men certainly have changed in the last 15 years. Caught in the existential impasse, they're stymied by age, bald spots, their marital status, their fear of disease. Beware of the man who wears his hair parted low on the ear, fear worse the man who won't take off his hat! The modern single man wears mortality like perfume: 20 seconds into meeting a guy, he's writing his epitaph.

"I'd rather have been a cowboy than a therapist." Harry tells me. At least his sports coat was nice.

How does it happen, the flick of the switch we call "relationship?" What's the chemistry that changes two strangers splitting a pecan pie into a man and woman reconstructing a life? After meeting Harry and Melvin, I wonder, what did Rashi mean when he said that to a widow, two bodies are always better than one?

"Making a successful match is as difficult as parting the Red Sea," the rabbis report (in the Talmudic tractate Sotah 2a). It was hard enough when we were young, wasn't it? All that sweating and panting obscured potentially disasterous incompatibility. But if hormones are somehow less important the second time around, the magic is hastened if a fellow can remember my daughter's name.

"You're lucky he's dead," says my friend Gail, divorced some years ago. She means, assuming I had to be left alone, it's better to be a widow.

"People feel sorry for widows. They'll fix you up," says Gail. "But the divorced are failures."

She's right about this much: death is cleaner and there are no custody disputes. But the rivalry between the divorced and widowed is a color war between middle levels of Hell, a matter of degree not of kind. One lives in never-ending anger or resentment, the other in a state of permanent, yet exaggerated triumph. Like the squabbling of gnats, it's a waste: Living in the past is a drag.

It's a black-tie affair and I am going with a ghost. My husband is being honored posthumously by an organization he once headed. I am dressed as Coretta Scott King, a living testimonial to a great man's work. I greet old friends; receive a plaque. His truth is marching on.

What kind of widow do they see? Do I project the Martyred Widow, living in weeds, feeding off memory?

The monied Merry Widow, exploiting with a vengeance inherited wealth? The Married Widow, seeking another Mr. Right to repeat the old pattern, hoping for history to repeat itself? Worse yet, the deadly Black Widow, with a web that ensnares and then kills? Where is Rhett Butler now, waiting to scandalize half of Atlanta by asking the widow to dance?

I look out at the dance floor, feeling, for once, completely transparent. My husband's buddies look at me, but see only him, or perhaps it is their wives they are thinking of, here alone some years hence. As I set my smile to approximate perfect affirmation, I think, Jackie Kennedy was smart. By marrying Onassis she spared herself a lifetime of unveilings and school openings in JFK's name. She insisted on her right to continue on her own terms.

Don't think it's so easy. The weight of the world, the weight of sheer being, holds you back. In Italy the women, dressed in black, sit like crows on their apartment house steps. Why don't they marry again? The truth is, if you must consider it, that patriarchal society expects and encourages a woman once married to live the rest of her life in memorial to a man. It is unseemly to recover too soon.

On the other hand, it is wretched not to recover at all. I think often these days of the first days when I was a bride, and how little I understood what I was about to undertake. I had a partner. I had company. I had someone to fight with who, even if he slammed out the door, was committed to coming back. It was divine.

And now it's over. No matter how you slice it, a widow's life remains a hobbled one. It's unnatural to live on, echoing forever a song already sung. A life as a museum, as if a woman could have no purpose on her own. For good reason did the prophets lump the widowed with the wretched, the fatherless, and those without legal status. We are dependent, if only upon memory and a life now gone.

February 1988

One Year

Burton was buried in his best pinstriped wool suit, white cotton shirt and my favorite of his red and blue silk paisley ties. In his shirt pocket as always was his gold ballpoint pen. On his fourth finger, left hand, was his wedding ring. On his feet were black wool socks.

A full year after his death, this is what amazes me: How difficult it has been to put the past to rest, how against nature it is to say farewell. By the way I dressed my husband 24 hours after his last breath had gone, nuzzling my cheek against the lapel of his suit in a gesture of *au revoir, mon amour*, before handing it to the mortician, you'd never guess I don't believe in life after death.

You'd think that I think Burton could return some day, and would have to go to the courthouse immediately before stopping off at home for a shower and change of clothes. I even brought along his newest black loafers, but the dead, the mortician told me, wear no shoes.

So maybe I do believe, in a peculiar way, in the possibility of resurrection. Not that I seriously considered that one day a Messiah would lift the dead bodily from their graves, pinstriped suits and all. But neither could I entirely dismiss it.

Was this why I had promptly rejected cremation, despised as it is by Jewish tradition? Burned to a crisp, I'd never recognize him in the hereafter.

(Ancient Israel, by the way, had no such illusions. The Hebrews left the body above ground a full year until the flesh withered and only the bones remained before being finally interred.)

Hope and desire still stirred within me. Anyway, wherever Burton was heading, he should be nicely dressed.

It really is bizarre, the way we wish and hope for the impossible. A month after the funeral, I hoped for a phone call. Later, for a letter. Wherever Burton was, wouldn't he at least write to tell me he'd arrived safely?

And maybe he actually did. There was that dream, after all. Dead only two weeks, Burton appeared to me while I slept one night; he was skipping around trees in a park as I picnicked nearby. It was a spring day; he was happy and looked fit in a checked shirt and jeans.

These moments add up, instincts more than intentions, pointing out that however much we want to let go, memory is like Velcro, by which we cling to the land of nevermore.

We have finally returned to the gravesite. A month before yahrzeit (the year anniversary) there now are 22 of us, not 300, paying tribute. The gaping wound where the earth was cut for Burton's casket has filled in with grass. Brown paper approximately two by four feet lies over the marker. We are here for the unveiling.

Jewish law requires erection of a monument after death, but the ceremony to unveil that marker is only *minhag*, or custom, celebrated some time before the end of the first year.

I resisted coming back here. I knew what it meant: The year is over. After the unveiling, I will no longer be a mourner, standing in the depot between death and life, honoring both the ephemeral and the Divine. "Life is eternal; and love is immortal," a poet explains, "and death is only a horizon; and a horizon is nothing save the limit of our sight."

Over, finished forever, except in my heart. As I cross the lawn to the spot beneath the cypress tree where Burton lies, I am afraid.

"The Lord is my shepherd, I shall not want," we begin. We recite the Kaddish of course, and the *Malei Rachamim,* the prayer for the departed. "God, full of compassion, grant perfect rest to my husband who has gone to his eternal home."

Now Samantha and her friend Ariel, ages 6 and 7 1/2, rise to uncover the tablet.

So small. So neat. So still. Though I'd ordered it myself, I feel a jolt of disappointment. Had I expected a last-minute surprise appearance? A puff of smoke and a genie with a magic lamp?

"The dead speak through their silence," the rabbi says. We read the tablet with Burt's name. "Devoted Husband and Father," it reads. "A Gift for Laughter."

It's nice. A little symbol of the scales of justice fits between the dates of his existence, 1930-1987, symbolizing a man of law. But from five feet away, the plaque is indistinguishable from any other; from 10 yards it is clear that, lawyer or no, here lies just one more of the dead.

"The unveiling puts a period on the end of the sentence," my Aunt Libby told me after she had mourned my Uncle Bernie. Yes, it's true. In the end, Burton was a man like any other, incapable of reversing the inevitable.

I'm not a widow any more, and let's drink to that. At home, my friends and I eat and go down to the garden to plant an orange tree.

It is time to plant. I dig my shovel deep into the dirt and throw it on the tender root ball of the Valencia, praying only that the tree one day will bear fruit. I pass the shovel to Samantha who digs in too, and she passes it to Michael, who passes it to Willie, who passes it on to...

And so a new sentence begins.

May, 1988

Making Memories

Aunt Rose's earrings sit in an old cardboard jewelry box. Some are encrusted with fake diamonds, others are festooned with pearls or tiny ceramic flowrs. Cheap stuff, but I've always loved them. Last year, when guadiness was in style, I wore them to go out at night.

Aunt Rose was Grandpa's second wife, and you know how these things can be. My one memory of her was her sick bed. She wore a floral silk bathrobe and her dark wavy hair was lacquered under a net. She handed me a long wooden stick with a tiny hand on the end and let me scratch her back. Her hands were shiny with oil and her neck smelled of sweet cologne.

A few weeks later, she died; I was seven. We went to her house and the family picked over the cut-glass bowls and figurines that were her legacy. That's how I got the earrings, through my mother, years later.

When you're not left with much, what you have must do. I think a lot these days about memory, how it serves us, how it fails. Six-year-old Samantha misses her daddy. Amidst the weight of all he has left behind, I search for the tiny prop, the gilt earrings or back scratcher, that might do the trick.

"Let me have my privacy, Mommy," she says. She closes her door.

"Daddy," I hear her say. "I have a friend, A-, you don't know her. And I have a new cat, Charlotte. I'm different now."

In the beginning, after Burton died, Samantha often would take out the family videotapes and rerun her old birthday parties. Or, she'd go to the drawer and play with a Chinese fan he brought for her from San Francisco.

But now, a year later, the white bathrobe he gave her is too small and the tangible, physical presence is going, too.

"I saw my daddy today in the clouds," she says, almost too poetically. "But then the clouds blew down to Mexico."

Some days, when her school work is finished, and "La Bamba" has played a hundred times, a look comes over her. Then, we sit on her alphabet bedspread, lean against the blue and white wallpaper with the mural of cows and ducks and take a trip down Memory Lane: to the swimming pool where Daddy threw her into the air; to the egg salad sandwiches he'd make her for school; to the time the ambulance came for Burton and the driver wouldn't let her go in, too.

We both know what we're doing, making tracks in the soil of disappointed love. We visit the fire department and the paramedics who once saved his life. We play doctor, nurse and patient. We try new cures. Sometimes we come home alive.

"Daddy loved me, didn't he?" she asks. Finally, when even Samantha finds this all intolerable, we read *The Trumpet of the Swan* and go on.

What do I want Samantha to remember? What would I just as soon have her forget? What tyranny will the past have on her? And what truths will she choose to never know or recognize?

I'm cleaning out my garage, hoping to remodel. A large dumpster sits outside, waiting for my verdict: which of the 40-odd Bekins boxes shall live, which shall die. These are the remains of my husband's office: he never threw away even an electricity bill or a parking ticket, let alone a message from a client. Telephone message pads and diaries from 1968 on, are all in order. Every memo — maybe 300 of them — he sent in 1972 to a law clerk or secretary is neatly filed away.

I sit in my jeans on the concrete floor, ferreting through the boxes. I am, reluctantly, self-appointed curator of a bizarre museum, preserving I'm not sure exactly what, for I'm not sure exactly whom. What innocuous tidbit — the check stub on a crucial date, a Rolodex card — might Samantha eventually need from these archives to keep her soul afloat?

Well, that's what I'm doing here, isn't it? Engaging in prophylactic resuscitation, trying to save Burton once again from the dead, this time in response to a child's need. I can't create a legacy of experience for her any more — her dad is dead. So I create a legacy of record which might one day light her way.

But let's be honest; the process hurts. How little it is that we actually leave behind, even the most prolific of us. And upon close inspection, that little bit amounts to what? Even in a life of purpose and achievement, it's shocking, truly, the junk with which our moments are filled. The head spins in a renewed grief when measuring the minimal effect of it all. In all these files is there nothing worthy of a "Movie of the Week?"

In the Shesh Zecherot, the six daily remembrances which are part of morning prayer, we learn the high art of facing facts. In a history of 4,000 years so replete with experience, record and drama we are commanded to remember only six events, including both the good and the bad: the Exodus from Egypt, the revelation at Sinai, our harassment by Amalek and the forging of the Golden Calf, the slander of Miriam against Moses and the celebration of the Shabbat.

It's a curious listing, but makes sense. A legacy is not an aimless mass of papers thrown at our children: it is a selective process in search of significance. And significance comes from seeing a life cleanly and whole, assigning responsibility to the man, his world, his enemies and his God.

It is chutzpah to sculpt from these boxes an expurgated version of Burton's life. But am I dignifying his memory by allowing the fat to subsume the meat? The alternative is to save everything and leave Samantha to wander through her father's trivial pursuits to find the true legacy of record, so valuable and so dear, that he left behind.

Life needs space. A relatively few pages out of all his work — the symbolic equivalent of an earring in a cardboard box — reflects the man I knew, and the snap, crackle and pop which his daughter has, too.

This is his legacy and when the garage is cleared out, it will be plain to see. May his memory be for a blessing.

June, 1988

Taking off The Rings

We bought the rings on my lunch hour. The engagement ring has a plain, round-shaped diamond in a platinum setting; the matching wedding band, nestled like a flower against a leaf, has three tiny diamond chips. I was 24, it was the height of the women's movement, and as a purported anti-materialist, I was outwardly blase about the whole deal. Yet, for the first year, I had a lot of manicures, and whenever I looked at my left hand I registered the thrill of reconfirmation that I was connected to another through law and love.

Over 15 years I sometimes imagined throwing the rings at him and walking away. Ultimately, they've been off my hand only three times, for cleaning. These rings have caught on my stockings, pulled on my sweaters, attached to stray threads as I glanced by. But they are a part of me.

The summer after the funeral, I met a scholarly man at a summer retreat who seemed interested in me. It took me weeks to realize that he spent a lot of time looking down at my hand. Anyway, I came home and removed the rings from my fourth finger, left hand, to my fourth finger, right hand, a step at freedom. Samantha noticed immediately. "Your ring!" she exclaimed. My hand felt cold, naked.

But recently, a nice guy asked me: Can I love again? Will my first marriage lie there on my right hand like a puppet with a voice, holding strings against my future? So, it's clear that soon the rings must go. I'm single now.

I'm not up to it. I seem to have lost all my skills. Basic

innate instincts of good judgment are gone. But what criteria does a man or woman choose a mate? What values beyond passion must we consider?

My friends warn me that now I'm particularly vulnerable. They mean, I'm vulnerable to easy kindness, to simple concern, to the projection of my own desires onto an unknowing passerby. The young widow: My father says, be careful, men will take advantage of you.

They're right. I can make big mistakes.

Recently I met S. He was tall, imposing, with a beard and glasses, he wore a blue suit and a nifty bow tie. The moon was full, the stars were out. I was away on business. He was away on business. We met on line at the smorgasbord. His first words were, "Don't leave me."

What is it like, to feel something for a man after all this time? Terrific! Sane! Treasonous! Like an ice cube down a sunburned back, I shiver in the heat.

We took a walk. We stood by a fountain, and sat on the lawn and picked at the grass. For a moment, all the stars were in conjunction, just as it says in the Zohar: "The divine, the angelic, the human, the vegetable and the animal powers will all be in harmony."

When he kissed me, he said, "I've known you forever." And did I ever want it to be so. After all, the perfect union of man and woman hastens the Messiah.

I have been wandering in the desert of "wantlessness," daring to dream of a future. His words for me were like rain. Oh to have desire born again, to take the gift, the risk, the glory of moving on.

Of course we talked about a future, though we live thousands of miles apart. He promised much, I wanted much. There are a lot of angry women who have been sold a bill of goods by men who get carried away. Men who promise women everything, but can't follow through. My answer is: It takes two to tango.

It takes one to promise, and another to believe the promises. It takes one to say, "Gee, it might be fun to raise a 6-year-old." And another to think, "Yeah, and maybe you're the right guy for the job." It takes two who yearn for completion to follow each other out on a limb, carrying a two-handed saw.

The problem is not the size of our promises — we all promise more than we can deliver — but where they come from.

The Kabbalists tell us that there are two levels of living: the "garment" level and the "soul" level. The "garment" level is all the outside effect, the suit, the beard, the moonlight, the one-way ticket out of loneliness that sells a man and a woman on each other. You can fill a whole closet with garments and still feel naked.

Real love is on the "soul" level. On the soul level there are no empty promises, there is only commitment; there are no false appearances, only transparent knowing of each other and a shared destiny.

So eight hours was a nice beginning. And the ring is off for good now. One day, the Messiah will come.

July, 1988

Part Two
Family Life

"He who learns from his elders,
what is he like?
Like one who eats ripe grapes
and drinks old wine."

Sayings of the Fathers

Queen for a Day

It will tell you all you really need to know about the town of Delray Beach, Florida, where my parents "snowbird" each year from December through April, to say that the most popular hair and nail salon in the area is called "New York Hair."

Most everyone at New York Hair is not only from New York, but even better, many are from Long Island, and even more particularly from my home town of Plainview. This is no coincidence. Delray has been razed and rebuilt to look so much like any flat Northeastern suburb that when we first visited Delray some years ago, my husband passed the shopping center on the left and the temple on the right and said, "I think we're here."

"So you're from California now? How do you like it?" my mother's friend Ruth is asking. Mom and Ruth never actually knew each other in Plainview, but at New York Hair they're buddies.

"What's not to like?" my mother answers for me. Mom and I are sitting on adjoining bridge chairs before matching white tables, getting manicures. If there is a greater mother-daughter thrill than shopping and lunch, it is this, sitting side-by-side with our fingers soaking in hot water. The heat of our all years together evaporates in pleasure.

My mother is having French tips, little white crescents painted on a pink base, and why shouldn't she splurge? Tonight is her sixty-fifth birthday party. She is Queen For A Day and I am the visiting dignitary.

Ruth takes out her wallet and passes a photo.

"Did you know my son Steven? He graduated high school a year after you."

The photo is of a man who could be a dentist, in his late thirty's, with a dark mustache. I shrug my shoulders.

"They all look like this," I say.

"My boys did very well for themselves," Ruth continues. "Even the younger one — he lived in India six years. Today, God bless him, he's in real estate."

When my father announced he wanted to retire, you could have blown me over with the proverbial feather. My grandfather worked until he was nearly eighty. Adlers never rest.

"You're not insulted?" my mother had asked, when they bought their condo in Delray. Some people move to be with the grandchildren.

I told her then what she had told me when I first moved out to L.A. "Whatever makes you happy." I guess I meant it, but I also meant what I didn't say: Damn it. A lifetime spent changing planes in Atlanta lay before me, and then what?

"I don't know," she had said, "I guess I'm not a pioneer. I don't want to make new friends. I don't want to find a beauty parlor by myself. I don't want to be dependent on you." Of the sixty guests at her party tonight, I've know more than one-third all my life, including Mimi, my one-time neighbor from across the street. All of them now live in Florida.

The truth is, my parents are happy, but me? I'm still holding my breath, fearing they'll get immediately old. I guess they know this, because whenever I speak to them, they offer the complete lowdown of their activities: See how busy we are? This is not at all "the elephant's graveyard," as the mean-spirited call Florida.

When I go there to visit, my father plays the piano,

my mother shows me her photography and tells me about her clients (she's a financial planner specializing in seniors). It's a little like visiting day in summer camp, but should a hint of this float across my face they look at me as if to say, "Hey, we're entitled."

My father was a salesman, a big success at providing industrial supplies to Long Island's growing manufacturing plants. He hated the road, he hated the grind. He liked the paycheck. For 20 years he had been looking for a way out.

My mother waited 20 years for a way in. Thwarted at every step by selfish males — a father and older brothers, then by bosses who paid her little — she saw less motivated men get educated while she, talented and energetic, typed envelope labels at home. Work was joy. Work was freedom. Even if it was beneath her, she was glad to be of use.

On my mother's birthday eight years ago, my parents were in a head-on collision on a country road 10 miles from the nail salon. They'd been out looking for condos, and made the wrong right turn. When my brother and I scavenged through the demolished rented car, retrieving my mother's calendar diary and her gold bracelet, we saw the dent made by her head in the dashboard.

But when Mom awoke from her near-coma with a battered face and a ruptured heart lining, she immediately announced she was going to go to college; she graduated with honors four years later. I could show you the picture.

My mother's artful investment of my father's savings allowed them to sell their small business. Her skill fills me with pride.

And still — perhaps you can detect this — their retirement has upset my expectations. I thought that life was about working ceaselessly, struggling until the day you drop. Where did I learn this, if not from them? I look at my parents today and see another possibility: a story with a happy, open end.

February, 1989

Four Men

In recent months more than a few friends and acquaintances have asked me, as nicely as they can, why a wonderful woman like me isn't married.

"Surely there are many eligible men who would appreciate a person such as yourself," they say, or variations on this theme. It seems inconceivable to them, especially if they've been married any number of years, that someone as terrific as I am hasn't already made my match, and so they begin to think I'm being "selfish," purposely depriving a lucky man of my company. Surely I'm too picky. Too demanding. That I'm once again expecting a Man on a White Horse, instead of just an honest Joe.

I scarcely know what to say. Is a single woman really "selfish" for remaining unmarried? Am I refusing to look hard enough for a possible mate and thereby truly "depriving" a man of the "good wife" he deserves? Somehow, I thought conversations (and newspaper columns) like this went out with the 20 cent stamp and the VW bug.

Still, why not address the question directly: why am I not married? Part of it is choice, part luck and chemistry, of course, but there's something else. Fact is, it's taken me a little while, several years of being alone, before I understood today's men.

What is there to know? Maybe it's the impact of this Passover season, but I've come to see that in the single world there are four kinds of men, comparable to the Four Children who, during the Passover seder, ask the

Four Questions. The Four Questions are supposed to tell the story of why and how the Israelites were freed from slavery in Egypt, but let's not be too literal.

These Four Single Men have their own styles, quirks and ways of coping with their reality. When it comes to the question, why am I not married, they evoke Four Different Responses (as the sages would say.) They are: The Divorced Man, the Widower, the Never-Married Man, and the Man About Whose Status it is Best Not to Ask..

The Divorced Man:

Gary is a divorced man who insisted he is ready to start over. So he invited me to dinner; I ordered a salad, but it reminded him of his wife Caesar's. My Honda reminded him of his wife's Jag. I was talkative, which reminded him that his wife was silent.

To the Divorced Man, you must say: forget your ex-wife! all single women are not out to belittle you, to take you to the cleaners or otherwise restore you to the diminished worm you were at home with her! (A variation on the Divorced Man is the Too Newly Divorced Man, who'll take you out to dinner, as Jan did me, on the very day he signed his property settlement agreement, and then complain that you eat too much.) With a mighty hand and an outstretched arm was the single woman spared from falling in love with a man newly divorced.

The Widower:

Steve's wife had died suddenly. Bitter, cursing his God, he told me "I can live without Brenda, and I can live without you." But his bitterness and sense of powerlessness stopped him from seeing that I was hurting, too. The Widower, more than the Divorced Man, the Never-Married Man and the Man About Whose Status it is Best Not to Ask, has the greatest chance of loving fully, once he heals. But unlike the Divorced Man, he wants exactly what he had before, down to the color nail polish, the saintly Wife who Died. He needs to recognize that he is part of a community of tragedy, and that life has gone on.

The Widower needs to be told, it is because of my own memories that I cannot get married yet. Because of my memories, not because of you.

The Never-Married Man:

The Never-Married Man does not realize that he has given up hope. He says he has not met "the right girl yet" and asks the single woman "Who are you?" as if being single is her fault, and he was God's gift come to save her. George, never married, likes to tell women on a first date what's the matter with them. "Remember," he told me, "Angels can fly because they take themselves lightly."

To the Never-Married Man you must say, it is because of what the Eternal did for me that I was spared love with a man who believes in his own deity.

The Man About Whose Status it is Best Not to Ask:

Of the 10 plagues which afflict the Single Woman (about them on another occasion), falling for a man about whose status it is best not to ask is one of the greatest. He may be married, pretending to be single, or in any event the victim of a shrewish, insensitive woman (who will not let him go.) He maybe divorced but still in love with his ex-wife (or his mother.) Lenny lives in a trailer on the same property where his ex-wife, daughter and the ex's new husband live in a house Lenny bought her. Such a man has no capacity for commitment, but makes a big show of love. He'll pull the rug out from under you.

To *The Man About Whose Status it is Best Not to Ask:* you must say, if I never meet another man about whose status it is best not to ask as long as I live, *dayenu.*

Of course, there are Four Single Women, too, but no one asked about them.

April, 1989

Give Me a Minute

Mike had read the *One Minute Manager* and the *One Minute Salesman* so now he hoped to become the "One Minute Casanova."

"Listen," he says to me on the phone. "I'm a businessman, so let's be efficient about this. We'll meet for coffee, let's schedule, say 20 minutes. O.K.? I mean, you'll know and I'll know in 20 minutes what we have between us. And if we like what we see, then we make a date."

Usually it take me more than 20 minutes to pick out my earrings, but I figure, what the heck? Mike has convinced me already that he is everything I could want in a man, so I am ready to be impressed.

But then...Mike is sitting at a window table not far from the door when I arrive.

"Hi!" I say, and as I walk toward him he ever so furtively checks his watch. Twenty minutes later this is what we have between us: two drained coffee cups and a small arugala salad. The fork hasn't had time to defrost when he shakes his head.

"I'm sorry," Mike says sadly. 'There's just no magic here. I know magic when I see it. This isn't magic."

Do you think I make these stories up? Recently, I met Bruce, an attorney with a toupee. Anther quick study. Two short dates and he had big plans.

"So what do you think of our relationship?" he asks.

"Relationship? This isn't a relationship, Bruce, it's only lunch."

In dating these days, time is of the essence and attention is focused on the bottom line.

"Is he worth the effort?" a friend asks about a possible fix-up. Who can be bothered with merely a nice dinner, or a guy in a nice suit? I say, people should come to first dates with letters of reference from three close friends. Maybe Mike, the "One Minute Casanova," is cruel, but he isn't so off base. In 20 minutes either there's magic or there isn't, and hey, baby, life is tough.

Two years have passed since my husband died. The jacarandas are in bloom again. With a halo of blue flowers on green feathery leaves, the jacarandas were in flower the month my husband lay dying, and by the time of his funeral, blue petals littered the streets, trailing out cortege.

"Have you always been so tough?" my friend Ed asks. Who knows? The year Burt died I cracked four teeth, but inside I never broke. "We are survivors," my mother tells me, "You're not made of spit." Of course not. But a few weeks ago, in a moment of whimsy, my brother and I had our tarot cards read on Venice Beach. "You are in a period of transition," said Mya, looking at a card of a woman by a boat. "Don't choose pain."

Well, of course I am recovered now. I've had new loves, new dreams. I have heard "our song" on the radio and couldn't recall why I once like it. And yet... the other day, a note came from my synagogue, which caught me up short.

"Dear Marlene," it began, with a neat black handwriting filling in the appropriate blanks.

"We are called upon to remind you that the yahrzeit of your beloved husband..." How tough am I if a form letter from a synagogue can register shock?

When I was a child, the scariest night of the year was not Halloween, the scariest night was when my mother lit the yahrzeit candles, in memory of her parents. Once a year, the flames flickered for 24 hours through the cheap glass jelly jar with the paper label, casting color shadows on the kitchen walls, announcing to us, night and day, that the dead, for all their silence, must be served.

The question is, how to serve and how much? What is eternal and what is irrelevant? For a while I obsess about what is the true memorial date, May 14, the day he died, or the fourteenth day of the Hebrew month of Iyar, which varies by the year? Obsessing about detail can be therapeutic, a last ditch attempt to hold on.

"I never knew my mother's Hebrew date," my mother tells me. The news comes as a relief. I can fudge a little, no one will tell.

"Weep ye not in excess for the dead," said the prophet Jeremiah, "neither bemoan him too much." There is a myth about mourning, that it ends at some finite time, that one heals in a year, and then goes on, embracing the new.

No, it doesn't happen that way. The dead linger with us, eternal in our hearts, and there is no healing from their loss. Those who go through it know differently: the spirit heals in its own time. It may take a week to go back to work, and two months to feel like dancing at a wedding. But it may take years to reform a full life, to feel that the feet are standing firmly on the ground. Oh, if only I could be so kind to myself, to believe the words I just said.

Life continues, as we wish it or not. We do go on to new experience, to other lives. But that which is part of us remains forever, capable of tugging at the heart strings at odd moments, as long as we live.

But time does heal. A tragedy recedes; a candle is lit, a story earns its 20 minutes, and we wait for the jacaranda to bloom.

April, 1989

Fishing Expedition

For all my talk about self-sufficiency, there are times when I do miss having a man around the house.

Last week, at the start of her summer vacation, Samantha popped the question, "Mom, can we go fishing?" and the thought of her Dad came into view.

Burton hated fishing, and warned me when first we met that he'd never set foot in boat. The last time he'd ventured out to sea was in on a fishing expedition off Baja California. He'd try to be one of the macho guys, an Ernest Hemingway sort. But there he was, minutes out of port, vomiting overboard. I know he would have answered her question with an immediate and not-guilty "no."

I, on the other hand, am the New Woman and the New Woman can never say no to activities usually associated with men. As it is, angling was the playwright Lillian Hellman's favorite sport, but I never claimed it as mine. Nevertheless, soon I stood, rented pole and bag of bait in hand on the local sports fishing pier, surrounded by guys with tattoos, beer bellies and women in bikini tops standing around as happy ornamentation. Refusing to acknowledge the obvious smirks around me, I manfully speared an anchovy onto a hook, only to find it disintegrate into my hand.

"Do you know how to fish?" a skeptical Samantha asks.

"Sure, nothing to it," I say. Fearlessly, I stab another anchovy in the guts and head, thinking sadly of Caesar salad, then watch with sinking heart as the bait falls off the hook as soon as it hits the water.

"Can you help my Mom?" Samantha asks a guy whose arm says "Rosie, Kathy, Iris and Fran." "She's not doing so well." I shrank as he deftly loaded the hook, then threw the reel back over his head and let 'er rip what seemed like several hundred feet into the sea.

"Sorry," says Rosie, Kathy, "I lost your bait. It's too mushy. Anyway, there's nothing to catch today." By day's end, we were comrades in the struggle, for he too was empty handed, and his smirk was gone.

I've learned a lot about men from having to become one: the stress of being sole breadwinner; the burden of exuding confidence when I feel doubt; the mixed bag that comes with being the ultimate authority on home wiring.

The other day, I introduced my girlfriend C to what I refer to as "my husband." It's a gadget, about six inches long, half an inch wide and it has a top which expands and contracts. Don't blush. What it does is open bottles of any size mouth, from ketchup to mayonnaise, hooking on to the edge and twisting to release the cap.

Having this efficient opener around our all-female household has made me wonder how history would have been altered had all women inherited a "husband" like mine. After all, my mother taught that men are for opening bottles, (how effortlessly they tap, tap, tap the knife on the rim) and that only they know how to break the vacuum seal which locks flavor in, as the ad used to say. What will technology think of next?

When a woman becomes a Single Mom, she automatically becomes adept at opening bottles, baiting fish hooks and rewiring old lamps. No other choice. Still, however competent she may look in her mirror, Single Mom inevitably becomes an object of pity to men.

Young and old long to take care of her and her little one, to wrap the two orphans (Mom becomes an orphan too, by this scenario) up in their brave black cape and sweep them to safe. They know that underneath our strong exteriors, we're really nincompoops.

Samantha and I have met them at the hardware store, guys who can't bear the thought of a woman on a ladder. A woman with a plumbing snake positively makes them shiver. I have a master's degree: theoretically, I'm as capable of putting in a new hanging lamp as any guy with a tattoo. But somehow I'm presumed to be a complete idiot the minute I get a hammer or a pair of pliers in my hand.

It's not just tools and fishing rods: even intellectual men, the kind who can't change a sink washer, assume that single moms are a danger to themselves and their children. In their minds, all order is gone from our lives: only they can separate us from the tidal wave of oncoming chaos.

Some months ago, Samantha and I spent the morning with friends. Art, a well-meaning man I'd never met, was part of the crowd. He took one look at Samantha, all dolled up in her plaid dress with white collar, and found the child he was meant to have.

By the time we finished our bagels, Art was insisting that he should become Samantha's "big brother."

"You know," he said, "I can take her to the ball game, and stuff." But when he came to dinner the next week, and saw her struggling with her real-life homework, he promptly had second thoughts.

It's pretty seductive at first, having complete strangers fall for me and my kid. It confirms that, however nuts things may seem at home, to the outside world we still give off a Madonna and Child appeal.

But like all idolatry, worship is not the same as love. They're falling for an image of themselves, not a sense of me and my chocolate pudding/fish stick kind of life. And anyway, it doesn't occur to them that, whatever it may appear to be, Samantha and I are doing just fine.

I'm not against falling in love with a real guy. And I'm not against a man having an interest in our ready made family. But compared to baiting a fishing hook, landing a guy is not the first skill on my mind.

July, 1990

Crying Uncle

We all need families of course; the link between generations keeps us from floating in an abyss of alienation.

But it is nevertheless true that there is an ugly side to family life. Envy, jealousy, competition — this is what we learn at the familial hearth, alongside love, sharing and waiting your turn for the bathroom. We all want to be Number One in the eyes of our parents, and this primitive urge, this basic drive, which continues on through adult life, is why the family, perhaps more than any other human institution, is the vortex of emotion and passion. The family resists civilization, and is too often ruled by the law of the jungle. Only a fool would mistake the desire for and the love of children with the sometimes sorry relations between grown-up fathers and sons, mothers and daughters. Generation after generation, the blood never learns from its mistakes. It's a wonder we don't kill each other more often.

These thoughts have been with me since around Memorial Day this year, when my father received a phone call.

"Jack, it's me. Murray." For 13 years, we had not heard a word from my father's youngest brother. Murray's absence lingered like an amputated leg. He was missing, but he was not gone. Not hardly. We noticed what Murray did not do — the gifts he did not send, the condolences he did not offer — just as we might have noticed what he did do, had he been around. My father would grimace with disappointment and I learned from his heavy heart that all the best wishes in the world could not put some things right.

"I have cancer," Murray said now. So he was coming back to us after all. On October 1, Murray died. And 17 days later, in a bizarre coincidence echoing eerily of wish fulfillment, his apparently-healthy wife Roberta died too.

What is there about families that makes good beginnings go sour?

Murray had been my favorite uncle on my father's side. "Gotcha nose!" was the game he played with us children, winning our eternal devotion. When he married Roberta, I was their flower girl, carrying my basket down the aisle the year Grace Kelly married the Prince of Monaco. I was in love with them both. He was my father's handsome "kid" brother, almost a kid himself with a broad open face and clear friendly eyes. He was our future, and anything seemed possible.

Childhood is no augerer of character. Only few years later, Murray and his father had a fight over — what else, money — and when he was ultimately left out of Pop's will, he played the sullen role of Esau, vowing retribution against his three brothers and sister for his missing birthright. But how could Murray get justice from them? Only Pop could make him whole, and he of course was gone.

"What a waste!" my father would say. He was visiting Murray every week now in the hospital, watching his fine, athletic form deteriorate into an old man.

"He still talks about the money! He still insists on his innocence!" As the oldest surviving member of the clan, my father was now, reluctantly, the stand-in for Pop.

"Murray, forget it!" Jack said. "I forgive you. We all forgive you. It's too late for this now!" Dad's despair was mounting, and even from my distance, I could feel the anger, too. Murray, damn it, had dropped back into his life, bringing with him not only the old love, the old hate, but the old responsibility, too. Who would sit *shiva* for you, old buddy, if you did not come to me?

Through it all, Jack would not turn away, and would only say, "What a waste!"

There's nothing new about any of this, of course. Brothers parting. It's a story as old as the biblical Jacob, as eternal as Arthur Miller. As right on as Barry Levinson's new movie, *Avalon*, about family love gone wrong.

When we were children, my brother and I, watching the internecine spectacle of our family bloodletting, promised each other we would never part.

"This will never happen to us," we said. Hope it won't.

November, 1990

Ellis Island

Despite moderate showers and a gray, unappealing fog, there was nevertheless a two hour wait for the Circle Line boat to Ellis Island when Samantha and I arrived some time after noon at Battery Park during Thanksgiving weekend.

A two hour wait means about 3,000 people; there are three ferries an hour, each carrying an average 900 people making the 25 minute triangular trip from Lower Manhattan to the Statue of Liberty and then to the island itself, home of the newly renovated and reopened Ellis Island Immigration Museum. With winter's early sunset, the last boat ($6 for adults, $3 for children) leaves Battery Park at 3 p.m., but the crowds — respectful, orderly — keep coming well into dark, emerging out of surprisingly clean, well-lit subways (!), to gaze from New York's southernmost edge at the unobstructed view of Liberty as her golden Torch is lit, perhaps to gain a shot of inspiration from this site where America opened up. There is a holy place in New York City, but until this last visit I knew it not.

I am here on a mission, re-staking the family claim. A few weeks ago my cousin, M, came to L.A and we met, after more than two decades separation, with our respective children near the teacups at Disneyland. I think we were both pleased and surprised to make a reconnection and to find that family ties might still hold.

We were bounding up and down the Swiss Family Robinson when M announced, almost in passing, that the family had decided to list our grandfather among the

"Ellis Island Historical Notables." The brainchild of Lee Iacocca, chairman of the Ellis Island restoration, this meant that for a fee, the name Samuel Adler would be inscribed in bronze among the list of those millions who had passed through Ellis Island during the heyday of American immigration, roughly 1892-1924.

"What a great idea," I said immediately, wishing I'd thought of it first. "How much does it cost?"

"I think it's $100," said M, becoming a little uneasy.

"Terrific. How much do you want?"

"It's already taken care of," said M, now averting my eyes entirely. "I called all the male cousins, and they each contributed $20."

"The male cousins?"

"Well, yes. It was sort of a 'male bonding' kind of experience for us."

I passed the last gurney of ropes from the tree house and came down the Swiss Family to solid ground.

Male bonding. Oh brother.

I let it go, but not for long. A few weeks later my brother called.

"I told M to call you," Alan said, when I confronted him about the plaque. "I said I'm sure that this is the kind of thing you'd want to do too."

And how did my youngest cousin N feel about this Ellis Island tribute?

"I felt dismissed," she said, elegantly. About a tribute to our grandmother Mollie, (dead before any of the grandchildren could meet her) no one said a word.

I was still smarting over the Ellis Island plaque, when, in conversation with my aunt Rita, (my grandfather's only daughter) I came upon another bit of family trivia: not only had been one there been three sons who made it safely to America, but there was a sister, too. No one knew much about Sam Adler's sister, not even her name, but it was clear she had not come from Russia with the others, and perhaps never came at all.

By the time I arrived at the ferry slip at Battery Park, I was in a snit; the world was out to get (and forget) women, always had, always would. I imagined my unnamed great aunt had died a horrendous death in a pogrom, a victim of both the czar and her brothers' neglect. My own grandmother, brought over to America by her husband Sam, would disappear without a trace, no plaque to commemorate her journey, while my grandfather's tribute was memorialized via a male ritual like a beer commercial. The unfairness of existence overwhelmed me and it was only my daughter's request that I buy her a green sponge liberty hat which brought me back to earth.

"Mommy, she's beautiful," Samantha said, looking out at Liberty, now less than 500 yards away. Indeed she was, and the quiet sight of her looking out toward Europe as we passed on, was as soothing as a maternal kiss on the brow. Come on, she said, aren't you being silly? Our ferry was now leisurely retracing the precise route that Sam (1910) and Mollie, three or so years later, had traveled. Mercifully, no tour guide announced the fact, so that when it came upon me, it had the force of an epiphany.

"This is the route Grandpa's father took when he came to this country," I told my daughter, for the first time truly inspired. "Can you imagine it?"

Once on shore, we did the normal tourist things, imagining that the grandparents were along with us. The Ellis Island Immigration Museum is a huge open hall, a canvas purposely left blank for the modern imagination. There are the beautiful authentic Victorian lighting fixtures and clerestory windows, but the metal railings which herded the immigrants through massive lines (as many as five thousand came a day during my grandfather's era) are gone.

There are also three stories of exhibition rooms and Samantha and I went through the processing center and the medical room and the various holding facilities. By the end, we had an inkling of what it might have been like to become a cog in the immigration mill. No wonder Grandpa never mentioned Ellis Island again.

Did he think he was heroic? Was he merely glad to be escaping Russia and certain service in the Czar's Army? In fact, my grandfather's generation wasn't exactly the heroic type. They thought in terms of self-interest, not as sacrificial vignettes ala a Movie of the Week We think they're brave because we are so grateful, and because the story turned out so well.

And finally we visited the sea wall. The name Samuel Adler will be about one-quarter inch high; there may be 20 or more panels each about four feet tall for names beginning AD-AG alone. Still, the view is nice. I think I'll enroll Grandma Mollie myself.

On the return leg of the trip, the fog had lifted and the Manhattan skyline lay before us. I could imagine the city as my grandparents had seen it long ago and feel some of their hope as well. It was a troubled country when they arrived, after all, but they did what they could.

And as for Sam's nameless sister, the Cossacks didn't get her after all. She moved to Israel, I've been told. One day, I'll have to look her up.

December, 1990

The Two of Us

"Mommy, can we go visit Frank Sinatra?"

The singer is building a house a few miles from us, but Samantha, age 9, knows nothing about this. My daughter has a big, Broadway-style voice and somehow has become convinced that Sinatra can help her.

"I want to go on tour with him," she says confidently. "If he hears my voice, he'll let me sing with him."

Childish hubris? No, it's more than that. When we're driving in the car, she asks for the Sinatra tape.

"Come fly with me, let's fly, let's fly away" we begin, swinging with Nelson Riddle's orchestra until Samantha interrupts.

"Mo-ther, did Sinatra ask you to join him?" she says curtly. She's right. My voice is terrible, but that's not the point. Samantha is entering the stage of competition. For weeks now she's been watching me like a hawk, examining how I put on make-up, which shoes go with what skirts.

"Who's prettier?" she'll ask before we go out. In this cram course on young womanhood, my every act is under a microscope. She mimics my voice on the telephone; she studies what music I listen to when I'm happy, and which when I'm at a loss. In every act she's anxious both to do me proud and to out-do me altogether.

So with Sinatra. With no Dad in our house, Samantha needs a prince to compete for, so now she'll fight with me over who "wins" the heart of The Chairman of the Board. All normal, said Freud, all normal.

Of course, it has to be like this: The war between the

sexes goes on whether or not the primary male is present.

"When am I going to get a new Daddy," she asks, sometimes more fervently than others. It's not only that she misses her own father, (though the ache has not abated, not so much as by an inch even after four years), it's that she yearns for a steady, anchoring Maleness in her life, an Otherness by which to set her stars. Security attached to a deep voice.

A few months ago she thought we'd found him. The New Daddy. I was dating W., and one night at the last minute I had no sitter, so I had no choice but to bring Samantha along.

He was charming. She was charming. He told jokes. She laughed at his jokes. They were a wonderful pair. I went to the bathroom while he paid the bill. When I returned she was whispering to W.

"He doesn't have a wife!" she called out before I got to my seat. I looked at them both. "Do you hear me? He doesn't have wife!" She kissed him when we left, and cried on the way home.

She wants a Daddy. The normality of this yearning has been hard for me to accept. Don't I climb up on the ladder to change light bulbs just like he used to? Don't I rewire lamps and fix broken stereos?

But whenever I point this out to her, making explicit how well we two are getting along, she'll blurt out "This house is falling apart!" And of course I know what she means. Last year, I could with justification maintain that I was both Mom and Dad to my daughter. From my vantage point, I did it all. But this year, when the body is changing and boys won't be caught dead on her softball team, the truth is harder to take. I am Mom. Maybe a great mom, even SuperMom. But Daddy I am not.

Well, O.K. We don't have a Daddy. But the fact is, and even Samantha can sometimes see this, it's not so bad.

Being with a Mom who only pretends to be a Dad has its benefits.

We walk around the house without our clothes on. We can fantasize about the new Daddy she might want. A Daddy who can pitch softball. Or a Daddy who can pitch the perfect tent.

A real Daddy might be something else again.

Things were going along pretty well with W. until some weeks later, the deluge. That's when Samantha got a whiff of what the future might bring. She was riding in W.'s car when it happened. He was listening to opera. She wanted KROQ.

"If you don't change the station right now, I'll never speak to you again," she said, trying him on for size.

"Fine," he answered, just like any Daddy would do. The opera stayed on. And just like any Daddy, he didn't speak to her for three hours.

"Mommy," she said the next day. "I like it just the two of us." I plugged in the Sinatra tape and when I began to sing, she didn't stop me.

May, 1992

Toolbox

I come from a long line of plumbers.

Both my mother's brother and brother-in-law were union men during the building boom on Long Island; they laid the pipe across what was once potato fields bringing civilization to towns like Levittown and Westbury, at a time when doing manual labor was no shame. My husband's step-father and step-brother were plumbers too, some 3,000 miles away across the country, and my husband himself spent the summer up to his elbows in grease, unclogging drains while waiting for law school to begin.

Being plumbers by day, the men in my family were do-it-yourselfers at night and the weekend. My father made the furniture in the family playroom, put up the knotty-pine paneling, installed the overhead lighting. My husband ran the wiring for our stereo system through the walls and up the attic and down again.

One of the main things my father and husband agreed on is the importance of a working garbage disposal. "Don't skimp on parts!" was a commandment they both obeyed. One year, while my parents were visiting, the preschool had a dinner and the sink got stopped up. My father and husband spent much of the evening together in the school kitchen, one of them under the cabinet, the other above, maneuvering the faucet, happily endeavoring to get the water to run free.

From this I observed a lesson: real men do it with tools.

I don't remember ever seeing my mother near a hammer, or even change a light bulb. A woman's job is directing, not repairing. She watches from afar, standing back in a critical mode, saying "more to the left, no to the right, no back to the left," while he tries to hang a 30-pound picture frame on the bedroom wall.

My husband used to complain that his mother made him push the grand piano back and forth across the living room until she found the perfect place for it to rest. But after we got married he moved that piano often, even eagerly, for me.

The natural division of labor dictates that a woman stands and waits as a willing lieutenant, holding the ladder, the open box of nails or the hammer while the screwdriver is in use, acting only if a man asks for help.

You'd think, given this background, that my father would have been apoplectic with fear for my future after my husband died. Nothing doing. Soon after we came home from the funeral, my father set about taking inventory on my husband's tool chest.

"You know he left you a full set of wrenches," Dad said approvingly. He knew from then on that I'd be in good shape.

And it has been true. Over the years I've come to do more-or-less adequately some of the tasks I'd spent a lifetime watching men perform. I can rewire a lamp! I can find the two-by four-studs so a wall doesn't shrivel into plaster as soon as the nail goes in. I still can't fix a garbage disposal, but I'm working on it.

There are so many tools in my toolbox: Hammers of five sizes and weights, screwdrivers both flathead and Phillips, the wrenches of course, and the pliers. It's a good set. I have no tools, however, for what needs fixing on this and every other Father's Day. No hammers, nails, wood, pliers or wrenches can make a Dad where there is none.

We have become matter-of-fact about it, Samantha and

I. The first miserable year, I tried to get a jump on things. When the other first-graders made paper cards for "Dad," my daughter addressed hers to Grandpa and Uncle Alan. Two gifts for two men, to make up for the one man who was gone.

"Father's Day, oh bro-ther!" Samantha said the other day, when she heard a department store advertisement on the radio. By now we're not exactly relaxed about this loss, but at least I didn't have to stop the car for mutual consolation. This year, while other families are exchanging ties, we'll go to the zoo, and have a nice dinner and maybe buy some new recycling bins for our home. Much like my husband would have done.

In my tool chest, I see now, there is another appliance, one I'd never valued before. It's the gizmo which lets me appreciate the "Dad" qualities where they appear, even in myself, and to value the men and women who have been there for Samantha and me in "fathering" ways.

There are the fathers who show up at the Little League games each week, rooting for the whole team not just their own child's playing. "Go for it, Samantha!" they shout, as if my little girl was their own. And when the game is over, one or two of them have been there, with a pat on the head, or a signed softball symbolizing victory. We can't have enough of these guys, even if some of them are women.

June, 1992

Missing Pieces

God works in mysterious ways. I'd been alone for any number of months, spring bleeding benignly into summer. Suddenly, I was back to reading Sara Paretsky thrillers and renting a lot of Bette Davis movies. Then the phone rang. It was my lawyer, C.

"Do you date?" C. asked.

I held my breath, knowing C. was irresistible, but very married.

"What do you mean?"

"I have a friend you should meet. The energy will be very good. Can I give him your number?"

A blind date! Now I know what you're thinking, but you're wrong. From the right source, a fix-up carries the endorsement of angels. Be trusting, I told myself as I drove into the parking lot for our first lunch. And I knew by the crease in his tweed slacks and the shine of his prematurely gray hair as I saw what I could only hope would be him sweep into the restaurant ahead of me, that he had not only read but absorbed Deborah Tannen's *You Just Don't Understand* (which explains why men and women can't talk to each other) but that he would like grilled eggplant.

O.K. I was a bit eager. But from the first moment, it seemed so... so right. The careers were so parallel. The vocabulary, so similar. We each had young daughters!! Here was what Shel Silverstein calls "the missing piece." I met his colleagues and they wondered how long we'd been married. We caught a glance in the mirror: what a perfect couple! We took out the calendars and began to plot dates. I told myself I was too wise to be swept off my feet, but suddenly the ground below seemed slippery. And sure enough, pretty soon I fell.

Why don't relationships work? Everyone I know is looking for answers. Is it Los Angeles? The AIDS crisis? The narcissism of the '90s? Was there a problem in the parenting we received way back when that leads otherwise successful beings to become commitment-phobic?

But no, it was none of these. Even in this relationship created in Heaven, what was missing was ... it's awful to say it, courage. The courage not to get carried away, but rather to go slow.

To undertake love, you have to have confidence that you can pull it off. It's a risk, and readiness is all. The heart has been on the lookout even if the head is turned the other way. But it's easy to fool yourself.

Just one of those things, you say. Heady, exciting; for a while I thought of buying a strapless dress. Then, from nowhere, came dissatisfaction. With so much riding on each other, our whole lives seemed at stake. He said I reminded him of G; I said he argued like a lawyer.

"You're cold," he said.

"You're demanding," I answered. And suddenly it was too late. How odd, the way experience can make us not wise, but scared.

Perfection is never enough. There are no perfect couples, anyway, merely more-or-less compatible individuals willing to give each other the time of their lives. No matter how much we had in common, no matter how many obvious similarities and mutual points of reference, at the basic level this we did not have.

"It's too hard," he told me. I guess he was right about that, too.

August, 1992

Nothing to It

This was to be the year I built my own sukkah, a "hut" in which to celebrate the fall harvest festival of Succot.

Last year, I borrowed a sukkah "kit" which was designed and constructed by a friend. For eight days, as the Jewish festival of the fall harvest requires, I had dinner in this jerry-built hut, inviting friends to share an evening out under the stars.

Even my most skeptical companions found the holiday irresistible; they enjoyed the outdoor picnics eaten by candlelight, though more than one rationalist refused to shake the lulav branches (which joins together four species of plant), alongside the etrog, which is a variation on the lemon. They found in the shaking-and-waving ritual a primitivism which was embarrassing; it made them feel like Indians doing a war dance.

Still, it was our first true Succot, filled night after night with camaraderie and interesting conversation. Both Samantha and I loved it.

And so, this year I thought, I'd build the hut myself. What could be so difficult?

Armed with Michael Strassfeld's informative book *The Jewish Holidays,* I went down to the local hardware store. I'd been reviewing Strassfeld's sukkah plan for years and it seemed simpler (not to mention less expensive) than last year's version and something I could handle without much effort.

"The easiest way to build a sukkah is with cement blocks..." Strassfeld begins. The guy behind the counter at the hardware store eyed the book suspiciously when I told him I needed help.

"I'm building a hut," I declared.

"A hut?"

"Yes, I have the plans right here. It only has to stand up for eight days."

"Maybe you should see Ron, in the lumber yard."

Ron, too, eyed me with curiosity, as if this was a covert plan to remodel my home without a building permit.

"You're going to need to pour a foundation," he said.

"A foundation? It's supposed to be flimsy."

"Flimsy."

"Yes. We're pretending to be wandering in the desert, and these are the buildings we are living in. No inside. No outside. It's an insecure structure, and you're supposed to feel it swaying in the breeze."

Ron could care less. "Listen, lady. When the guys from the movie business build their sets on location, it's only for a day or two. But they build it tight and right."

"But I don't want to pour concrete. It says here I can just put the 2x4 wood posts into cement blocks."

"Cement blocks? Listen lady. Your friends are going to sit under the roof, right? You're going to have a table, and people will sit at it. Now just imagine a wind come along and the walls fall on them. They'll sue you."

"Sue me? I'm inviting them for dinner."

"I don't care. If the roof falls on them, they won't take it lightly."

Deep in disappointment, I went home. It just didn't make sense. The sukkah had to have a roof, true, covered with heavy cuttings of leaves called shkakh. But it was a see-through roof, with slats big enough to see the stars. If I made it too formal, the whole point of the sukkah, it's inherent fragility, would be lost.

Finally, I thought, what did Ron know? Jews had been building sukkahs for 5,000 years. No one pours concrete foundations. As far as I knew, the walls had never fallen on a single soul.

Just in the nick of time, my friend P. came by with his truck. He'd never built a sukkah before, but he had a spare hour and, hey, how difficult could it be?

This time we by-passed Ron entirely, and went straight to Robert, a bearded good-old boy from Wyoming. The look he gave us when we said we were building a hut need not be described.

I bought four 2x4s, six sheets of ready-made trellis for the walls, a box of three-inch nails, a new heavy-duty hammer and shovel and assorted odds and ends. The bill for this eight-day wonder was $178.

Feeling broke but unbowed, we got the home. Fifteen minutes into the building process, P. stood up.

"Gotta go now. Bye."

I looked about. There was one post standing upright inside a concrete block. Nails, wood, trellis were scattered over the lawn.

"Com'on Samantha," I called, "we're going to build the sukkah." I heard strains of "Phantom of the Opera" coming from the living room.

"I'm practicing, mom. Can't you build it by yourself?"

"Sure I can. What can there be to it? But come help me."

"Music of the Night" resumed on the piano. I began to hammer nails into wood. It felt good. The nails went straight into the 2x4s. With each whack I said to myself, Nothing to it. Nothing to it at all.

When I had one wall of trellis attached to two eight-foot lengths of 2x4, Samantha came out to watch.

"Grab an end. We're going to move this baby and make the wall stand!"

"Mom, are you nuts?"

"You want a sukkah don't you?"

"Call Terry the handyman. I can't lift this end."

"Sure you can. One, two, three...."

We lifted the wall up on its end. Slowly, we maneuvered it 180 degrees, so it was perpendicular with the garage wall we were going to use as a support. I was bursting with pride. Samantha and I are building the first wall of our sukkah. A tradition we would continue year after y...

"O.K.," I said. "Now you hold your end, I'm going to put this post into the cement block."

The poor girl held on for dear life. Ready, set, lift.

I heaved my end up into the air, but just as the leg was ready to go into the cement block, the whole wood trellis fell flat on the floor. "Mommm. Now look what happened."

The next morning I called Terry the handyman. I'm buying a prefab kit, and Terry can put it up next year.

October, 1992

Libby

My mother has often called me "Libby," and I never objected to the accidental slip of the tongue that seems to occur at oddly intimate domestic moments: as I set the dinner table on my rare visits home, or when we are off driving in the car together to a market or clothing store.

Libby was my mother's younger sister, but that's not the half of it.

My mother was 12 when her mother died; Libby was eight. The mixture of dependency and responsibility was not an undiluted blessing. As adults they'd visit for hours, knitting sweaters with complicated cables and raglan sleeves and then go home and call each other, descend into argument, hang up on each other and the next the day process would begin again. "I like the bickering," my mother said. "It feels real." Libby was like my mother's second skin.

It was no surprise to me that I was called Libby many times last weekend when I returned to New York. It was Thanksgiving and we were often in the kitchen where the domestic memory plays loudest. But my cousin, Reva, reports that her father, Yale, has repeatedly called her Libby, too.

Libby died in late October. She was the only one in our family who could make a proper gravy from turkey drippings. I used to stand by her side and watch, but frankly I never got it. Something about the proportion of turkey renderings to corn starch to hot water was lost on me. Maybe I don't use enough pepper. Even without a wire whisk, her sauce came out smooth. A miracle. This year, my mother made the gravy. It was delicious but it broke my heart.

Libby's death was horrible, her rapid deterioration from cancer made all the worse by the fact that she was totally conscious of each assault on every bodily function right until the end. Not for her the blissful exit of coma. She was so alert, so persuasive in her descriptions of the battle within that even with her gone, it seemed at first as if the disease had a life of its own, that cancer still lurked about the old ranch house where she lived alone after Bernie died, hiding in the dresser drawer along with the fake toy gun intended to scare off intruders, or in the basement, waiting.

But, no, there was no disease. There was nothing. There was a bedroom set of furniture which goes to Lorraine, and the country music tapes that go to my mother. My brother got the blue cookie jar and I got a black and white snow-flake sweater. The rest, as they say, is silence.

Libby was like an older sister to me; she was my mother's first "child" after all. This "sister" feeling was only enhanced after Burt was gone. Bernie had died only years before, and they were just about the same age, only three years apart. This had unnerved Bernie, but it comforted Libby, oddly, when I became a widow, too. Finally, she had something in common with me, other than my mother, and in our shared grief she was the expert, having arrived there first. I was part of her sorority — the widow's group — and she expected me to understand things my mother could not, the pain of two a.m. in a lonely bed, or a New Year's Eve spent home with a book.

Age no longer was a boundary. When she called, we spoke in a kind of shorthand. "It's tough," she would say out of the blue. I'd know precisely what she meant.

When the cancer was initially diagnosed (already spread from the kidney to the brain), the first reaction was "Huh?" Libby was prepared to die of stroke, like her parents. Or complications of diabetes. So in addition to disbelief, the entire family felt cheated in its expectations, as if we had gotten off a plane at the wrong destination. Heredity, that mean-spirited determinant of all that lies ahead, had been an unreliable navigator. We were ready to blame overweight, or neglect of some kind. But this? What are we to say about this corrosion from within?

What we are to say, perhaps, is what my Uncle Bernie, Libby's husband, told her only a few hours before he suddenly dropped dead after running the track at the gym: "Man plans, and God laughs."

In Lorraine's kitchen last weekend, we sliced the turkey and warmed up the gravy.

"You know what I think?" Lorraine said. "Even if you eat the perfect diet, exercise daily and never have any raw sugar, you're adding four months to your life, at best."

My aunt liked: whipped cream, the company of family and old friends, good looking men, Chinese food. With Bernie gone, she met Frank, whose brother was a priest and learned to play golf. "He's good to me," she said. "And I'm not having any more children." She liked a good laugh and a story with a surprise ending.

I was out of the country when Libby died. I missed the funeral and the *shiva*, with the inevitable nervous noisiness of people walking on shaky ground. From a distance I heard only the grief of others; my mother's cries and my cousin's strength. I marveled that the gravy got made at all. At the dinner table, she was missing. And when my mother called me Libby, I flinched.

November, 1992

Gotta Match?

It's December, which, as every single woman knows, is the season of Get Me Out of Here! Every advertisement for scotch and diamonds and velvet is a living indictment of our singular status, every day closer to January is a confrontation with one's own deepest longing. Everything hurts, a kind of a pagan fear takes over as the solstice nears.

I'm on my own, living through December shadows. I notice everything: the way the sky feels at 4:30 as the dusk settles in; the way a Sunday morning stretches out into eternity making one and all think only of escaping into an early movie; and the way the year seems to be turning so fast, so fast, and I'm on the road to... where?

Which explains why this year, feeling Get Me Out of Here! with a vengeance, I drove at the urging of my friend C. to the office off Pico Blvd. of a bona fide full-time *yenta* whom I'll call Gittel. Yes, a matchmaker. I mean, why not? If you think about it, a matchmaker is the closest thing in our tradition to a "spiritual" woman, in touch with a higher power. She's doing God's work, after all, bringing a male and female together.

I imagined my *yenta* straight out of *Fiddler on the Roof*, babushka and all. She'll be just like the grandmother I never had; all knowing, all loving, wise in the ways of the modern shtetl. Within minutes of feeling my aura (I expected *yentas* to read auras) she'll say "Have I got a guy for you!" Such a thing did happen a few years ago, my friend A. She met her husband through the rabbi's wife of a minor Orthodox sect in Jerusalem. God works in mysterious ways, I thought. Even though I'm neither Orthodox nor living in Jerusalem, I figured Who knows?

Parking my car in a deserted shopping center near the appointed address, I wondered, Would she have a crystal ball? Would she have the Jewish equivalent of "Love Potion No. 9?"

"Fill this out," she said, offering me an application form on a brown clipboard and a seat on a vinyl covered chair. No crystal ball, here. There were two desks, a filing cabinet, a telephone and a rolodex: What more does a yenta need?

The form had 20 questions about my weight, education, and expectations in a man. What did I think was most important in a mate; Power? Ambition? Sense of humor? How would I describe myself: Sensitive? A work-a-holic? What did I consider an adequate income? \$15,000? More than \$80,000?

"What kind of guy are you looking for?" she asked, apparently unable to read my aura so early in the game.

"A guy who isn't starting therapy tomorrow," I said.

"A guy who isn't finding himself, you mean?"

"I mean a guy who isn't trying to be his own best friend, who isn't into 12-step programs. A guy who isn't into blaming his mother or has yet to make his career move."

"Sounds serious. What do you like to do on a date?"

"I hate to date," I said.

"You have to date. Tell me, what kind of relationship do you want?"

"I want exactly the kind of relationship I already had," I said.

"Well you had it already, why not try something else?"

"I want a life, not a date. I want what Hillary and Bill Clinton have. Can't I think big? I want to reorder foreign policy and work for social change, national child care and undoing twelve years of Reaganomics."

"You have a lot of energy," Gittel said. "I think you should try younger men."

Here is Gittel's wisdom:

#1: Matchmaking is a lot like direct mail advertising; there's a 2% rate of return rule of thumb. One hundred leads for every two prospects.

#2: In dating as in real estate, December is bad for everyone. No one closes the deal until after January.

#3: Finally, a bit of pragmatism.

"Don't look for love, look for friendship," said Gittel, "If you meet people with a closed palm, they'll walk away. With an open palm, at least you can shake."

Get Me Out of Here!

December, 1992

From a Distance

"Hey, Marlene. What's up?" My brother called a few weeks ago. His was more than an idle question.

"I got a message on my machine from Dad, and now he's not home. You know how often he calls me, so I figure something's wrong."

"You got me," I said. "No one's called here. You think we should call hospitals?" It sounds ridiculous, I know. After all, my parents could have been in Atlantic City for the weekend and my father was only calling to announce he'd hit a jackpot. Or they could have been gallery hopping near Alan's apartment and thought to drop by. It didn't have to be bad news, did it?

But in our nerve endings, a suspicion had lodged which would not let go. Alan and I have been learning to worry about our parents; to feel a threat of the ominous drifting through every innocent breeze.

"I'll call the neighbors and Uncle Yale," he said, "maybe they'll know. Call you right back."

My brother lives in Manhattan. Closer than me, but still, as it turns out, too far for many things. Much of our family is in Diaspora, scattered far and wide. I'd pondered this for a long time, ever since I moved to Los Angeles. Was I irresponsibly passing the buck to my younger sibling?

Mixed up in my thoughts were a host of clichés: that the daughter, not the son, has the primary burden of care for aging parents. That if you have two children, you want two children living near by. But lives are not reversible. Eventually, on whatever personal terms we desire, we cut free.

Over the years, a weight has lifted and the guilt eased. My grandfather spent his last 20 years in the same two-block area. But my folks travel around the country through Elderhostel and they snowbird each winter in Florida. No point in my staying home. If, God forbid, calamity is coming to us, I'll catch it on the run.

My parents still live most of the year in Long Island on the same street in the same house where we spent our teenage years. Many of the new generation of home-owners by now are young enough to be their children, and this generational surrogacy is an odd comfort for them and for me.

Marcia and Lee, who live in the house across the way where Mimi and Bob Levine once raised our friends Joan and Chuck, are devoted neighbors. They take in the mail and the newspaper when my parents are away for the weekend, and keep an eye out for burglars. That kind of thing. But now, as we began to sleuth down the clues of the parental whereabouts, neither Alan nor I had Marcia and Lee's phone number and we didn't remember their last name. Uncle Yale, who lives on the other side of town, and Lorraine, my cousin who lives in Westchester, didn't have a clue.

Alan and I sat close together on the phone lines, plotting; the 3,000 miles between us was obviated by dread. This, of course, is yet another reason people have more than one child: to save each of them from bearing moments like this alone.

We spoke to each other softly, with great care. I could measure what had been lost over the years of living in distant cities. My brother and I are no longer what we'd once been: so knowing I could tell his thoughts by a mere frown. But still, I could hear in his excited breathing a fear equal to my own over the big question hanging in the air. In our concern we were, for that moment, joined.

We called every hospital on Long Island forgetting until the last moment the one in our home town. In the end, that's where she was taken. It was a car crash. By the time we caught up with Dad waiting by Mom's bedside, the aura of crisis was over. Alan and I were many hours too late. We'd missed it all; the ambulance, the car unwrapped from the electrical pole; the woman who ran her car through the red light while my mother was in the way. The long night suffered by Dad, moving through the hours alone.

"She's fine," said my father. "That's all that matters." But Alan and I were weak from the struggle, from the not knowing, from the cryptic phone machine message that had said nothing even as it said all. From all we had not been there to do.

I made a lot of phone calls.

"Her feet are swelling," reported my father. "She's got some bruises, yes. But believe me, if I needed you I'd say so." Would he?

"Look, I'd tell you if it was necessary," Alan said, my eyes and ears. "She's coming home. She's fine."

I guessed that this was true. She did come home and life, somewhat limited by physical discomfort and healing, resumed.

"I still hurt," she said. "Can you believe this happened to me?"

From my distance, all alone, I wasn't sure. So I flew home. Even if I'd live on the moon, I'd have gone back, just to see for myself. Such is the fate of love.

She was standing up tall; he held me tight and then smiled. What was all the fuss about, you might wonder. But if you have to ask, you'll never know.

January, 1993

Breathing Room

The first postcard came yesterday.

"Dear Mommy," it said. "I had a nightmare last night and when I woke up there were tears on my cheeks. P.S. I'm having a great time at camp."

She is my only child. I am her only parent. I love her, it goes without saying, though how I love her does not. When she is away, as she is now for three weeks, at Camp Hess-Kramer, only a few miles up the coast in Malibu, I see her whole. A girl who hates spiders, loves Elvis and volleyball and worries (truly!) about why rebuilding Koreatown after the Rodney King riots is taking so long.

And because we are only two, so tightly webbed together I can sometimes feel her exhale, in her absence I see myself as well.

When Samantha is away, I make brownies *with* walnuts (she hates them), reclaim my clothes hanging in her closet, listen to National Public Radio news instead of 102.7, and put my life as Eternal Role Model on hold.

Families like ours — rarely heard of when I was growing up, but now part of the norm — are just like everyone else's families, only more so. Of course you don't believe that. Everyone has an opinion about single parent families, and basically it's bad. Especially if the single parent is a Mom.

(If you're a Dad, at least you've got a chance of retaining your sex appeal. See Nora Ephron's *Sleepless in Seattle*. In this movie, half of America's women want

Tom Hanks and his eight-year-old son.) But the general idea held by one and all is that, whether we are single parenting by choice or by hurt, we can't possibly be doing all right.

But — surprise — it's not so. Family life for Samantha and me means we sit at the smaller table at family-style restaurants, but other than that, you'd be amazed, really, how normal we are. We have really normal arguments, about television and homework and living up to your potential — just like you do. Our household, now that Samantha is 11, is just like yours — a pressure cooker with the flame on permanent high. She's a normal adolescent, bound and determined to do things her way. Which means that I, like every other parent of a normal adolescent, am deemed certifiably stupid, dull, tasteless. For now.

"Don't wear that Mom," she tells me when I go out on a date. "You look awful." She volunteers to put my lipstick on me, fearing I will smudge my teeth. And oddly enough, I sit down and hand her the case. Only yesterday I was the avant garde. She used to stand by the bathroom sink, her eyes glazed filled with admiration. Today, under her gaze, I feel my growing decrepitude, I have become a lost cause in the matter even of my own taste.

"Oh Mom!" she says so often now, her tone of disgust telling it all. But when she wants something really hot, it's off to my bureau she'll go.

Being alone together, in some ways we're not like other families. We are, often, like two people dancing in a very small closet, there's only so much room to turn. In large families, people can be shuffled like cards in a deck. A kid can play off Mom, or Dad, or his other siblings. For us, despite the affection of friends, relations, the dog, and the baby-sitter, still, in the heart, where it most counts, she is always playing off me, my expectations, demands, shortcomings. Wherever she looks, there is only me.

But this isn't all bad. Samantha and I can travel together for weeks at a time and not wish the other person dead. There are no food fights in the back seat of the car. Nor do I spend hours hoping Samantha will go to bed early so her father and I can have sex. Oh well. It's what you might call a mixed blessing.

A single-parent family is like living in a crowded tenement: not much privacy where it counts, too much where it doesn't.

Trying to avert my relentless surveillance, my daughter has learned to do things for herself. She makes her own lunch, has taken herself to the orthodontist, phoned the doctor when she didn't like a pimple on her face. When she was seven she "bought" her own ballet shoes, and had the store owner send me the bill. She knows the public librarian by name. For all this, she can't open a math book if I'm not home, and won't make her bed without my inquiry.

We are in the car, driving down the highway to the sleep-away camp bus. On the radio, the Beatles sing, "Ticket to Ride."

"I think I'm gonna be sad, I think it's today
The girl that's driving me mad is goin' away..."

But it's not true. Neither of us are going to be sad, today, or for the next few weeks. We both know that enough is enough. Samantha spent all year thinking of what she'll sing for the camp talent contest. As for me, I've spent 12 months thinking that camp brings out the best in her, and can't wait for her to get more.

"I'm not going to miss you this year," she says. But as we drive along, she eyes me steadily, fingering my upper arm, kneading the flesh. She's committing my corpus to memory. I think I'm gonna be sad...

In Summer, string beans, tomatoes and children should run free. In camp, Samantha will discover through her bunkmates a) that she does not own the world's ugliest swimsuit; b) that not having a younger sister is not so bad; c) that saying Grace After Meals makes her happy; d) that I am not the worst parent in the world.

Thank goodness for summer camp. And a little breathing room.

July, 1993

Fasting Forward

When I was a child, my father and I competed to see who could stay away from food longer on the sacred day of Yom Kippur. My Dad's a real pal. He always let me win.

Here's what I like about fasting: the beginning and the end. I start out at 10 a.m. with a feeling of self-righteousness and a unity with a people all trying to stay away from the refrigerator. About noon, as the rabbi completes his sermon, I'd swear I am wearing a halo; I admire everyone around me and think what a wonderful community I am part of.

But around 2 p.m., beginning after "Yizkhor" memorial service and continuing through the long afternoon, I have what might be called an epiphany, an insight into my spiritual existence. This insight, which becomes insistent during our synagogue panel discussion around 4 p.m., is that a hungry person cannot think. I ask myself, in the phrases of Isaiah, whether this is the fast that I have chosen, and what has this exercise in egoism to do with repairing the world?

By 6 p.m., I try to avoid anyone I like, lest I inadvertently throw a tantrum. By "Neilah," the service that marks sundown and the "closing of the gates" of Yom Kippur, I am semi-euphoric. I sing out "Eliyahu Hanavi," and hope with all my heart that when the prophet Elijah comes he will be carrying a blintz casserole and a side of sour cream.

Each year I learn it for certain: Hunger creates obsession; obsession leads to idolatry; idolatry leads of course to sin. So if you get hungry on Yom Kippur, go ahead and eat. Think of yourself as fighting crime.

Many one-time children of the '60s are critical of what they call "fashion show" Judaism. To them, the holy days are holy, and wearing clothing to impress the neighbors is frivolous and unseemly. So they don't go to synagogue at all, rather than lower their standards and participate in such tribal silliness.

Personally, I like the fashion show. I used to dream of bringing my husband to synagogue with me, to show off our family as we sat together, all in a row. Burt, of course, cared not a minute for my kind of bourgeois social sanctification, and less for religion. So I had to go myself. Better luck next time, I say.

But even alone, I can appreciate the parade going on before me, and my own role in it. I like looking up from the *al chet,* that litany of sins committed and omitted which I am confessing to with such heartiness, to see a well-matched plaid suit or a woman in a nifty hat. It lifts my heart to see someone wearing a pair of new suede shoes at the beginning of the Fall. I like to examine hem lines, and lapel widths. And to see a good-looking man in a well-cut sports coat. Am I terminally superficial? A thing of beauty is a joy forever. And while cut-offs and thongs were proper attire in the Ark, they have no place standing before it.

I suppose it's true, that when I was growing up, synagogues too often were the showcase of the *arrivistes*, the new middle class which used the synagogue to consolidate social power. Well-dressed wives of temple and men's club presidents would sit fanning themselves in the overheated sanctuary, their coats puffed up on their laps, boredom and make-up streaming down their faces.

But I look back on those days now with a kind of nostalgia. There's nothing wrong with being part of a communal ritual and trying to impress old friends. A synagogue, after all, is not only a place to converse with God, but to see friends, and be seen too. Of course I want everyone to like what I'm wearing, to think I'm looking well, doing well. They saw me when I was down, was that better? And as for getting a new outfit merely for services, well, what of it? The pious, I'm aware, do not bathe on this day, as part of a ritual or self-affliction. But to me, the Jewish calendar matters, and the Fall season of the Holy Days is a time of renewal, of one's wardrobe and oneself.

Finally, a last somber word about Yizkhor, the special prayers said in memory for the dead.

This is what I remember about Yizkhor as a child: Crowds of adults pressing into the synagogue sanctuary.

The women, their hair pinned with doilies, holding lacy handkerchiefs; the men with gray faces, putting on prayer shawls and skull caps.

A feeling of doom overtaking a community. A silence filled with dread.

Children waiting outside the synagogue, boys under one tree, girls under another.

The door opens; crowds of adults pouring out of the synagogue sanctuary.

My mother's lacy handkerchief, crumpled tightly into a ball. My father's ashen face.

Walking back into the house, my father tears a hunk of rye bread, throwing off caraway seeds onto the floor, breaking the fast.

My mother sits with her coffee cup, staring into space.

Today, for some of my friends, "Yizkhor" is Yom Kippur. They call to find out what time the services begins. They arrive 10 minutes before, leaving 10 minutes after. Once, I was critical of them, suspecting them of spiritual naivete. But this is my third year sitting inside the sanctuary during the memorial service for the dead. That which I never understood, I know intimately now: what goes on behind the door in 10 minutes is more than enough.

"Our days are like grass," we begin. "We shoot up like flowers that fade and die as the chill wind passes over them..." I hear wailing, keening, sniffling and the inhaling of deep breath. From the armored heart of everyday life, grief comes bursting out, afresh.

And so as I see it, Yom Kippur, finally, is not about food and fasting, or about fashion and community. It is the day of atonement, or as Michael Strassfeld writes, the Day of At-One-Ment, when we accept, whether as fiction or true, that fate indeed is hanging in the balance. "On Rosh Hashanah it is written, on Yom Kippur it is sealed." For a full day, I face myself, my life's journey, my yearnings and accomplishments, my faults and my future. And the dead will have their say.

I say the prayers and, as I invoke the names of loved ones now gone, I weep for myself, for my child, for hard years and a love too early gone.

But as it gets to be too much, I hear another's cry, and then another's. And soon I remember that all loss is essentially the same, and all of life is bravery. It is true, as Samson Raphael Hirsch says, "In this feeling of 'community' tears dry up."

When the service is over, I am starving. I think of my father, ripping at the rye bread. A bagel, a peach, a scrambled egg. The long afternoon awaits. Hmm...Should I? Why am I even thinking of it?!!!!

May your fast go easy.

September, 1993

Part Three
Food & Faith

"Love is sweet,
but it's nice to have bread with it."

Yiddish proverb

My Mother's Refrigerator

The big gap between my mother and me is not our positions on the ERA, single women or sex. The real gap between us is the Refrigerator Gap: what our refrigerators look like, who they're for, what we put into them. Our conflicting attitudes toward food in the home speak volumes about ourselves in the world.

I can describe my refrigerator in a word: empty. I may be a Jewish woman, a Jewish mother, but my kitchen has a goyish kopf. My family eats, as the sitcom says, "One Day at a Time," frequently from the take-out section of the market where I aim straight from work. Lots of times, being your typical fast-track boomer with child, we head for the sushi bar.

Despite the white wine chilling and the five kinds of mustard, when you open my Amana 22 the first thing you see is the light bulb.

My mother has a real refrigerator. A real refrigerator has leftovers. In her icebox, blue Corningware competes with yellow Tupperware filled with single servings of rolled cabbage, pepper steak, kugel (noodle and potato), meatballs, chopped liver: Jewish womb foods. Heads of iceberg and romaine are tossed on containers of sour cream and gefilte fish; jars of sauces and mustard balanced uneasily on wedges of plastic-wrapped cheese; sliced pickles, turkey and pastrami wrapped in white deli freezing paper; vegetables and fruit in Jiffy bags piled higgledy-piggledy.

Maybe I'm overstating the case but I've come to think that our refrigerators reflect the unspoken conflict of their owners regarding the role of a Jew in America.

My mother's refrigerator is operated on the "in case" premise of human motivation. She cooks for 12 in case you should want seconds later; in case friends drop by for dinner unannounced; in case a particular craving for some delicacy like pastrami should hit. You might say she doesn't like surprises.

For me, surprise is devoutly desired, though not always achieved. Certainly I'll always be able to find pastrami should I develop a craving — the big question is where will I go to get it? I search for the new in trendy restaurants, believing food is chic. If friends drop in, dinner is a mystery, for them and for me.

Our refrigerators also reflect our views on sin and temptation. My mother believes that to overeat is human and temporarily satisfying. Perennially on a diet, she would understand why the starving Esau sold his birthright to his conniving brother Jacob for a pot of stew.

But do you hide from sin, or confront it? My mother believes in confrontation, optimistically hoping that the next time stew is presented Esau will resist. By contrast, my refrigerator is positively Calvinist: What soul is tempted by celery and Perrier?

Finally, our refrigerators reflect conflicting attitudes toward men and our families. My mother believes that food is love, while I resist the notion that this is so.

My mother's refrigerator is the fullest expression of her heart. Love is abundance, love is never having to say "I don't have any." Love is knowing that even if she's not home for dinner, her husband (and children, when we lived with her) will look at the kosher salami and the pre-sliced cheese and hear her whispering in absentia: "What would you like, honey? I have everything."

Even when Samantha was very small, we ate out in restaurants more often than we ate home: each night a culinary adventure. Now as a single mom, I'm too tired to choose, and have learned to live on take out, stopping off for an order of chicken fingers for Samantha and a stuffed baked potato for myself. So much for personal choice

And yet I admit to some ambivalence. Sometimes I stand in front of my refrigerator and wonder if I'm at the right address. What's missing in my home that I have a refrigerator like this? Are some basic human needs for warmth and nurturing going unmet?

"The worst meal made by your mother is better than the best meal I eat in a restaurant," my father said on our last visit. Seeing he was serious, a lump formed in my throat.

Certainly my husband would never have said that about me. And hey, that's cool. I'm sophisticated: I've eaten in Paris and Rome. I can order in 10 languages. But still the question remains: If no one cooks, is the house less than a home? Is the repertoire of love curtailed? And what day to day activity of caring takes its place: balancing the checkbook? taking your spouse's clothes to the cleaners?

When my parents come to stay with me in Los Angeles, I have an anxiety attack over my refrigerator. I'd die before I'd let them see it in its naturally naked state.

Weeks before their arrival, I begin the shopping, the cooking, the stocking. I become obsessive, in the thrall of some primal urge. I buy seven cantaloupes so my mother can eat them with the half-gallon of cottage cheese. Maybe my father won't eat tuna, I'll get tomato herring. Does he still eat tomato herring? Maybe I should buy cream herring? But will the onions give him heartburn?

I don't rest until the light bulb is hidden, until the aluminum shelves are filled. For a few weeks out of the year, my refrigerator looks just like Mother's. I know it's crazy, it's suicide. But it feels like love.

September, 1987

Cantaloupe and Cottage Cheese

The all-purpose Jewish woman's lunch

1 large cantaloupe
1/2 pound container of cottage cheese

Slice the cantaloupe in half. Fill cavity with cottage cheese to taste. Some people fancy it up with sunflower seeds or granola. I like it simple. Enjoy.

Fear of Frying

Each Chanukah I ask myself, Why did I throw out my blender?

I'm ready now for the eight-day Feast of Latkes which is how a cook might legitimately think of this holiday of lights and gifts, and even as I buy the 10-pound bag of potatoes something in me keeps repeating, It's The Blender, Stupid.

I must have buried it somewhere in the garage or thrown it into a dumpster only days after buying my first Cuisinart, saying Good Riddance to its long tubular container with tiny curved knife blades at the bottom which defied cleaning and which reduced everything from cheese to jicama to a lumpy soup. Did I act too fast?

The blender was already being consigned to the culinary backwater by the time I got married, having been replaced by the crock-pot and the coffee grinder as the wedding gifts of choice. But Jewish cooks, I should have known, exist in a state of ambivalence to progress. We do not go forward without continually looking back. I still have several hand graters with a dozen different sized holes, and I try them out each year just to make sure. Sure that my knuckles still bleed, sure that the aluminum holes of the grater strangle and mangle the potato into a messy heap rather than the Cuisinart's uniform slivers; sure, in short, that history has had its say. Because the argument still rages, you know; even now there are aging relatives and friends who insist that the hand grater is superior for potato pancakes to anything you can plug into a wall. So now I know for sure. Only with bandaged fingers can I go on.

But the grater's not the half of it. After I'm done with the grater I take out my cookbooks and turn to the latke recipe, only to find these words (from Libby Hillman, whom my mother regards as the highest authority.) "Place a few slices of potatoes, onions, and one cup of water in the *blender* (italics mine)." And I am overcome with guilt. Not because I am not completely positive that my Cuisinart can do whatever the old blender can do (I use the steel blade of the food processor for smoother latkes, the grater for crunchy ones), but because I can't prove it. And without proof, all of life is conjecture, which is no good at all.

I've been making latkes for decades now, and you might think every burning question has been settled. If so, you don't know Jewish cooking, which is based on the premise that there is a better way to perform every task, which only your long-deceased grandmother knew. Complicating matters for us modern cooks is the sheer amount of new multi-cultural information. Family habits and eating styles which once seemed handed down with the Torah (sour cream, not apple sauce, should always be served with potato pancakes) are now merely matters of taste.

Latkes, for example, are an Ashkenazic tradition, coming from Eastern Europe, while Chanukah's Greek origins place it as a Sephardic festival. I learn from Jean Nathan's *The Jewish Holiday Kitchen* that the word latke itself probably derives from the Greek word for olive oil, most appropriate since olive oil was used by the Maccabees to purify their temple against Greek orders. But the Maccabees didn't eat latkes, they ate (as do Sephardic Jews today) something approximating *loukomades*, deep-fried donuts dipped in honey or powdered sugar.

So why latkes? Potato pancakes are a Jewish adaptation of a Ukranian Christmas specialty called *kartoflani platske*, usually eaten with goose. Cultural historians suspect that Polish Jews were trying to make good with potatoes what they didn't have in cheese. After all, the story goes that Judith served the Assyrian general Holofernes lots of cheese and wine before cutting off his head, assuring the Maccabean victory. Cheesecakes would have been suitable (and less greasy) but ricotta was not easy to get. As it was, goose fat was the "oil" of choice for latke-frying back in the old country and this, my friends, is where the death-defying taste among the Jewish people for gribenes, fried poultry fat, must have been born.

In my kitchen, Chanukah is an Ashkenazic celebration with increasing Sephardic influence, if only because I have overcome my fear of jelly donuts. Don't laugh. Until I discovered their Mediterranean link to Chanukah, I thought of donuts in general and powdered jelly donuts in particular as somehow the dessert equivalent of Waldorf salad — something Jews ate only after they were completely assimilated.

As for making donuts, this too seemed beyond me. There was the yeast, and the deep frying, and how do you get the jelly inside? But a few years ago, I could withstand the challenge no longer, and bought a spatter cover for my deep fryer and spent an afternoon mixing flour and yeast into dough balls, spooning jam into the dough (it's easy) and eating the results as soon as they were covered with sugar. Now I'm free at last. Fear of frying no more.

The grater, the blender, the doughnuts — you think this holiday is all fun? Even now these issues remain: Should I make the latkes in advance and freeze them? (They'll taste just as good, but the drama of presentation will be gone.) Should I use peeled potatoes? (Healthier but the pancakes will be darker.) How long must the potatoes be drained, and how dry? (Did I overdo it last year and is that why a batch burned? Should I bake them instead of frying? (Less cholesterol, I guess.)

Ah, questions, questions. And eight nights to answer them all.

December, 1993

Potato Kugel

(Latkes in a pan)

6 potatoes (peeled, grated)
2 eggs (beaten)
2 onions (chopped)
1 tablespoon salt
1/8 teaspoon pepper
1/2 cup matzoh meal
1 tablespoon shortening.

Pour 2 tablespoons of oil in pan and heat in oven. Mix all the ingredients and then add to pan. Pour another tablespoon of oil over top of ingredients. Bake 350° for one hour.

Kugel

Some recipes you think you can live without and then one day you wake up in a panic that your grandmother will die and you'll never again have her marble cake!

That's how it was with me and noodle kugel. The name is funny, so laugh if you must. Kugel, as the Borscht Belt comics said, starts with "k" and "k" words always get laughs. Chicken is funny. Kugel is funny. But making kugel is serious business.

Embedded in my psyche is the memory of a noodle kugel, probably the most politically-incorrect food in the repertoire, which is why I hadn't spent much time looking for it. Unforgivable in its use of fat, eggs, milk and cheese and utterly without whole grain. But when I smell kugel, I'm transported to a world I no longer know, which though poor in a financial sense was otherwise luxurious world in its lack of nutritional self-consciousness.

As it happens, this very schism over the meaning between rich and poor was played out each week in my childhood as my parents would take us down to the Lower East Side, ostensibly to visit my grandfather or to shop the bargains along Essex Street, but it was something more. We would make the whole miserable ride in bumper-to-bumper traffic, my father cursing at the inevitable car stalled in the right hand lane on the Kosciusko Bridge, the air wretched with the smell of burned eggs from the sulfur plant.

But as we got closer to Manhattan, my mother would lapse into silence.

"Your mother," my father would say in explanation. "She thinks this is Paradise. This is beautiful! I couldn't drag her away from here. If she had her way she'd be living right on Stanton Street today."

My mother would look out the window, at the crumbling brick high rises and the streets sweaty with urban life. "It's true," she would say. "I always felt it was all here."

She must have been my age at the time. I think I know how it felt. Poorer in some ways, for having been able to move on. She could register the loss in the ugly brick tenements and the cobblestone streets which were the rich playground of her childhood.

So this is what I think about when I consider kugel: history, progress, and the personal costs of both.

A kugel in the oven smells like — melted fat. And fat, of course, is history. Passé. Evil. A noodle coated with fat cooking at 325° for an hour and a half is not to be confused with pasta (though the effect on the arteries may be the same).

Let us compare noodle kugel with, say, its Italian brother, fettucini Alfredo. The fettucini (never spaghetti) is cooked al dente, practically raw. The butter is softened and coats each strand just so. The cream is added, but just enough. The hand-grated pecorino romano cheese (no longer does one use mere Parmesan) is daintily sprayed over the coated fettucini in a rapid flick of the wrist. A twist of fresh pepper. Quick, to the table. Voila! You hardly know you've cooked.

A noodle kugel is everything a pasta dish is not. Slow, long cooking. It smells of excess, richness, expectation. It inhabits a kitchen and lingers a while, like a friend sitting down for a comforting chat. A chef makes fettucini Alfredo, but your mother makes a noodle kugel — get the point?

As for the ingredients. Never use a fresh made pasta, no matter what the culinary elite suggest. Remember that you are cooking this as an exercise in sensory recall, not as an entry for the Wolfgang Puck Noodle Kugel Bakeoff. Using fresh pasta, you would miss the plastic crinkle as the vacuum seal of the yellow and orange Manischewitz egg noodle package is opened. No. No. No.

Now comes the tricky part, at least for me; the matter of taste. My memory of noodle kugel was buried so deep in the tectonic plates of childhood that I didn't even know I was looking for it. I didn't even think I liked noodle kugel at all, having invested all my culinary energy (especially around the spring holiday of Shavuot, where dairy products are a tradition) in perfecting the art of making blintzes.

I was lost. I have tried, by last count, half a dozen recipes for noodle kugel. None of them were right. I tried the one on the Manischewitz package. Too sweet. I tried my favorite synagogue cookbook, too bland. Finally I gave up.

"Mom, do you add raisins to your kugel?" I said.

"Never!"

"So what do you use?"

"I changed my recipe a few years ago. I use corn flake topping now. It's the best."

I was horrified. "You changed your recipe?"

"Yes, and I'll tell you something else. The key to a good kugel is water. Before you put it in the oven, the pan goes inside a basin filled with water. It cooks up like flan."

We had a long talk that night, about life and change. The noodle kugel from my childhood was not like fettucini alfredo at all. It was a *pareve* kugel, which can be eaten by kosher cooks with both meat or dairy foods. It had noodles, chopped onion, ground pepper, a few beaten eggs and was cooked until everything was crisp, almost hard.

"Don't make it," she advised. "Too much fat."

So I made my mother's new noodle kugel recipe, with the corn flake topping, which I cook as required in a larger pan filled with water. I like it fine.

February, 1994

Noodle Kugel

1 pound wide egg noodles
7 eggs
1 cup sugar
1 pint sour cream
3 cups milk
1 pound cottage cheese
1 teaspoon vanilla
1/4 teaspoon salt
1 stick butter

Cook noodles.

In a separate bowl, mix remaining ingredients. Add to cooked, drained noodles. Place in buttered baking pan. Topping: corn flakes rolled into crumbs. Sprinkle with 1/2 cup sugar mixed with 1 tablespoon cinnamon.

Place pan in larger baking pan filled halfway with water. Bake 1 1/2 hours at 325°.

Mandelbread

In this modern world of take-out French cuisine and microwavable pizza, there are still some tasks which one undertakes specifically because they are difficult to accomplish.

Wood carving, stained glass window-making, silver jewelry design, weaving of textiles, tending a rose garden, using a potter's wheel. Doing physical work helps us cope; it reflects the fact that even in the age of computers and cellular telephones, life is hard. Inter-ethnic wars, cities falling apart, a leadership vacuum you could drive a truck through, these we can not change. So we pick a challenge that is possible to meet just to prove that even in times of havoc we are not easily defeated. Something in which the instructions are not clear.

And so it is in my family that baking is an art. My mother raised me to take to cookie sheets and pie plates as a painter takes to the canvas, as a form of self-expression and personal catharsis having only little to do with the end result. "Cream the butter and sugar until the granules have dissolved," is the kind of inexplicit instruction in which a person can lose herself.

I think of my mother while baking: This woman who usually can simultaneously listen to music on the radio, watch a TV news show and read the newspaper, is transformed, hurtling herself into the Zen state of *samadhi*, in which the very terra-cotta tiled floor and floral wall covering of the kitchen disappears and she enters the pure spiritual high based on unity of body, mind and spirit. Rolling, pushing, stirring, measuring, hands masked in flour, eyes focused inward, she is beyond the reach of mortal conversation.

"Without eggs in the house, I am nothing," she told me recently. In her efforts, she is after a different, more sublime, kind of communication. All action is pointed to one goal, compelled toward completion by the yearning to say something through a finished art form which is good to eat.

Which brings us to mandelbread. To make the perfect mandelbread is to enter the world of the Kabbalist, a nether world outside time and space. It is baked twice and therefore it is not for the timid, the young or the weak of teeth. Just as the Sages say that one must reach 40 before beginning a study of mysticism, so it must (or should) say somewhere that a woman or man cannot begin to make mandelbread until the children have begun adolescence, the age by which one has come to accept the existence of failure in the universe.

"I make mandelbread," my mother says, "while I still have a shred of hope. When my sister was dying, I couldn't do it. I guess I didn't believe anymore. But when things are only merely bad, not completely futile, that's the time. That's why I always keep the almonds and walnuts around, just in case."

What my mother bakes, even more than the meals she cooks, emerges from a whole menu of emotional response. If she tells me that she spent last Thursday making a batch of rugelach, her fine cheese pastries which are baked in logs and then cut into inch-wide pieces while still hot from the oven, I know she's happily anticipating a happening of some kind, maybe a wedding, or a new baby in the family.

If it's taiglach (nut and bread balls baked in honey), she's preparing to send care packages to all of us for a sweet new year; her famous pineapple pudding and carrot muffins remain at home, awaiting a round of get-togethers when friends drop in. The happy baker is at hand.

Oh, but if it's mandelbread, the zweiback-type almond cookie, watch out. Mandelbread spells trouble, anxiety born of forces beyond her control. When I was a teenager with a new driver's license, leaving home to meet young men she didn't quite know or trust, it was mandelbread day after day after day.

These days, mandelbread is known as biscotti, and it has a kind of trendy cachet in coffee shops and restaurants across the country. Calling them biscotti gives these hard-crusted cookies an elite Italian air, much as calling raw meat steak tartar lifts it above mere hamburger. Still, to my family it is mandelbread, simple almond-flavored fare, and to call it anything else smacks of treason.

Mandelbread is the Wimbledon of Jewish baking; the crucible, the testing ground, separating the men from the boys, so to speak. Let me tell you, now that anyone can make a perfect pie-crust, thanks to the food processor, 4-H Clubs around the country are engaged in an Emperor's New Clothes-style pursuit. But mandelbread... here there is a real distinction to be made.

My mother's recipe is the best in America. It is crunchy and dry, part lemony, part sweet. It is perfect for dunking. She never uses coconut, and (this is her own creative inspiration) she uses lots of chocolate chips.

"It takes a full hour to make these cookies, even before baking," she warns. "When I want a project that I can dive into, something that will make me forget, that takes every bit of my concentration, this is it."

I'm giving you her recipe. Maybe you're having a rugelach day now, but by summer you never know.

Anne Adler's Mandelbread

1 1/2 cups flour
1 teaspoon vanilla
1/2 teaspoon salt
1 teaspoon baking powder
1 cup plus 2 teaspoon sugar
3 eggs lightly beaten
1 cup walnuts
3/4 cups sliced almonds
3/4 cups chocolate chips
2 teaspoons cinnamon
4 tablespoons corn oil

Add 1 cup sugar to beaten eggs. Mix together oil and vanilla, and then add flour, salt and baking powder. Blend in nuts and chips. Form into two mounds the thickness of a banana. Bake on greased cookie sheet in 350° oven for 30 minutes. Cool and cut into 1/2 inch slices.

Lower oven to 250°. Arrange slices on baking sheet. Sprinkle with cinnamon and remaining sugar. Brown for 10 minutes, then turn and sprinkle again with cinnamon and sugar and brown again for 10 minutes. Can be frozen or kept fresh in wax paper. Enjoy.

April, 1994

Food for Thought

There's a famous cooking story which goes like this:

A young woman asks her mother how to make a brisket. "First," says the mother, "you buy a whole brisket from the butcher and bring it home. Then, you immediately cut off the bottom end, which looks like a triangle, and throw it away. You put the remaining brisket in a roasting pan with spices, salt and pepper, on very high heat and braise the outside for about 15 minutes to sear the fat. Lower the heat and cook slowly for many hours with a little liquid (wine or catsup do nicely) and sliced onions, until the meat almost falls apart. That's how you make a brisket."

The young woman did as her mother said and for many years brought home the huge slab of beef, cut off the lower triangle and threw it away, before putting it into the roaster, and so on. The results were delicious, but the woman was puzzled. One day, her grandmother came to visit and saw the woman preparing brisket. Once again, she cut off the lower tip and threw it away.

"Why are you throwing away perfectly good meat?" the grandmother asked.

"That's what my mother told me to do. It's part of the ritual which makes the brisket so tasty."

"Ridiculous," said the older woman. "She saw me do the same thing for years. But I had a reason. I never had a pan big enough to hold a whole brisket, so I had to cut off the end so the meat would fit."

Here's a story of my own.

When I was a child, my mother made blintzes from

scratch, making a big batch for the freezer, enough to last a year.

Out came the huge black cast iron pan, the flour and eggs for the crepe batter and the farmer cheese for the filling. Then she took out two old linen dish towels and laid them on the kitchen counter. I could hear it from my bedroom: the sizzle of the batter gliding into the pan, then a huge bang of the pan against the table top as the crepe was flipped onto the towel. And finally a little sigh of satisfaction as the crepes piled up. Sizzle, bang, sigh. Sizzle, bang, sigh. In my memory, making blintzes was as arduous and treacherous as digging a ditch.

Even when I had my own family, I dared not try to make blintzes. I didn't have the right dish towels. And I wasn't "old" enough or strong enough to lift the heavy pan.

"Nonsense," said my husband, a crepe master of wide repute. And he started to show me. If the pan was well greased with melted butter, there was no bang at all, only the smooth gliding sound of a crepe falling onto wax paper.

"Stop!" I cried out. "This isn't right!" I went to the linen closet and took out two old clean pillow cases. I took the pan and started banging. "I don't have the linen towels, so these will have to do!"

The big questions of adult life are not so much about right and wrong. They are, more often, about cold versus warmth, meaning versus emptiness, freedom versus oppression, connection versus isolation. That's why I cook: to feel warm, have meaning, feel free and make connections, more often around holiday time, but whenever the feeling strikes. When I cook I feel certain something is going to happen. This is important because often in adult life nothing much happens, not for a long time at any rate, and sometimes what happens won't be good.

But with food there's always a chance. I will cook. You will eat. You will smile. I will be happy. Life can be a dream.

Some years ago, seemingly out of the blue, I started making gefilte fish. No one I knew had ever made it before, so it wasn't like I was following my grandmother's tradition or anything like that. And I had plenty else to do, believe me. Still, the inspiration could not be silenced. I needed a different kind of connection to Passover, a connection beyond intellect, one that had less to do with my own specific past, than to a world-weary shtetl gone for good. Fish, I thought. Jewish women once made their own fish. I will make my own fish, too.

It's amazing how these impulses take over, the compulsion to eat and cook ritual foods which have no intrinsic spiritual meaning. Beyond challah and matzah, no specific foods are commanded of Jews to eat. Many foods are forbidden, but where is it written that every Jewish function has chocolate chip rugelach and pound cake?

The fact is that food is ritual, or at least a lead-in to ritual, and without ritual we would continue to eat, but without eating, most rituals would die. That's why I respect those so-called delicatessen Jews whose only link is corned beef on rye or a good onion roll. Through their deli order they ask: Where do I fit in? What must I cut off? What can I carry along from the past? And do I have the right to throw out what is stale and seek something fresh? And these are the questions which count. Given half a chance, we can all be what we eat, and a good onion roll, even today, is hard to find.

Gefilte Fish

(written with the accent
as your grandmother would tell it to you.)

So I make fish, and this is what I learned. It is hard work. And not cheap. You start off thinking that it should only take two hours, but it takes all day. Nevertheless it's a task I love doing.

I use a mix of white fish, pike and carp (ask for six pounds finished, and extra heads and tails for the stock).

The Stock:

First you make a soup out of fish heads and tails, 2 stalks celery, sliced, 2 carrots sliced, and 5 sliced onions, 1 tablespoon salt. Cover with three quarts of water and bring to a boil.

The Fish:

Next, you make fluffy fish balls (like matzoh balls for soup). No, I don't grind it myself, nor is there a carp in my bathtub. The fish man grinds it for me. Do I feel guilty? Only as guilty as I feel that the meat man grinds my hamburger rather than making me kill the cow myself.

Mix the ground fish with 1 large finely ground onion, 4 eggs and 6 slices challah or 3 tablespoons matzoh meal with 1/2 cup water, 1 tablespoon salt and 1 teaspoon ground white pepper and 1/4 cup oil. Begin to form the egg-shaped balls (about a cup of fish mixture) and drop them into the stock. Moisten hands in ice water so they don't stick. Soon you will sweat, and your hands will shrivel from soaking in ice water, but at least the fish balls don't stick to you. Drop the fish balls into the hot stock. Add more sliced carrots on top. Cover and cook 1 1/2 hours.

Remove cover for the last half hour. Strain stock over fish. Chill. Serve on lettuce topped with fish broth and carrots.

Just as you're wondering why you're going through this sweaty ordeal, the magic begins. You feel the imaginary babushka on your head tying back your imaginary long dark hair. The walls of your American adobe home are replaced by the brick walls of the European ghetto and up on the roof you hear Isaac Stern and his violin. That night, everyone at your table will marvel how you, a modern career woman, have miraculously turned into a gefilte-fish maker of the 19th century. If you've made fresh horseradish, your guests may be moved to tears.

Your friends will smile.

You will smile.

Life will be a dream.

April, 1994

Holding on Tight

The treacheries of adolescence can turn even the most cynical parent into a true believer.

Why is it that some children become monsters while others grow to full moral height, a flower arcing naturally toward the sun? Last week, in a tiny office of Kehillat Israel in Pacific Palisades, another shift in the kaleidoscope:

Samantha, sweating with anxiety, met with the cantor for her first bat mitzvah lesson. Samantha walked in alone, a girl with long hair, new washed out blue denims and an orange booklet filled with *haftorah* blessings she will recite next February 19. And 45 minutes later, she emerged, a young woman with a deadline.

How does it happen? How does responsibility, authority, ownership of a tradition, and the feeling of membership become part of one's character? This is the beginning of the journey for her, but already a subtle reshaping has occurred. Months ago, the mention of bat mitzvah brought out a list of deejays who might perform. But now, while dreams of an all-day dance party certainly remain, she's wised up. She'll tell me about the party only *after* she's discussed the ritual.

I am feeling incomparably grateful and wary at the same time. Grateful because, as the Native American saying goes, it takes a whole village to raise a child and ours has been, by and large, a caring Jewish village. That's why Dan Quayle is wrong. A Dad is important. A Mom is important. But at a certain point in life, the earlier the better, a child learns that the world does not stop at his or her front door. Even if I weren't a single mom, encouraging my daughter up the tough ethical ladder of independent thought and action, I would still have need of the wise support of community, with its clear standards and unwavering belief in the eternal nature of its values, hugging us close, holding on tight.

The bat mitzvah lessons are many things at once: an arrival into young adulthood, a commitment to Jewish life, a beginning of autonomy over self and values. But even though I have raised her as Jewish child, warming her by the great hearth of our community and its historic legacy, I have no certainty that it will stick.

From the earliest years in synagogue preschool, through the recent summers at Jewish sleep away camp, I have done what a parent can do: provide the rich soil of relationships and environment in which joy and identity can grow.

But will they take? The mystery only grows. So here she is, slowly on her way. The light is dawning that a lot is riding on her. The choice is hers: she can thrive, but she can also rebel, you know.

At the moment, this need for belonging becomes more crucial by the day. I see her looking out of the corner of her eye: what kind of woman will I be? The world is filled with crazy choices: a nose-ring here, a tattoo or a dog-collar there. It's not a matter, as I once thought, of merely being "one's own person," but of being one's own person within a world that wants you.

I have to wonder what 11-year-old Robert Sandifer of Chicago might have made of the "village" Samantha lives in, and the bat mitzvah ceremony now weighing so heavily on her. Sandifer, nicknamed "Yummy" because he loved to eat sweets, was murdered in an apparent gangland reprisal; he himself had killed a 14-year-old neighbor who happened to walk onto her block while Robert was spraying it with bullets. At the funeral, attended by mothers dragging their youngsters past Sandifer's coffin as a warning of where gang life leads, an 18-year-old young man made this comment to a reporter: "Half the kids don't care if they live or die. Their mamas don't care about them. The police and society don't care. It's just one less boy to worry about."

Well, I tell myself that Samantha will never have cause to feel that way. But who knows? She is part of something large and caring, not one less child to worry about, but one more intense object of societal concern, a child expected to fulfill a prophecy in the world. In any event, it's better that she reject it, than that the world reject her.

I realize how bizarre this is, coming from me. For me, and much of my generation, independent living, independent thinking, are the hallmarks of a successful life. We rebelled against society's expectations, against the "guilt trip" of belonging, and the invasions of privacy from a Jewish community which, always and forever, puts all its hopes in its youth. But with the times and the breakdown of so much around me, the comfort, support, joy and authenticity through responsibility now offers precisely what my child needs at a crucial moment in her growth: firmly defined rules for becoming adult.

"I told her what was expected of her and the priorities that she'll have to set if this is to work," Cantor Chayim Frenkel told me after his meeting with Samantha.

"After all, this bat mitzvah isn't only about saying a few words in Hebrew. If that's all it was, you could forget it, who would care? But what I told her is more important, that what she's beginning now is the gateway toward the rest of her life. And that it's up to her."

What seems, after all, to be turning Samantha on, is how much there is to do that is only hers alone. "It's not your bat mitzvah," she tells me. You better believe it.

September, 1994

Planning the Party

Samantha is preparing for her bat mitzvah next February and, basically, it's been a pleasure.

Even now, she's on the couch in the living room with her orange booklet in hand, singing out her *haftorah* and Torah readings. We specifically picked a Torah *sedra* (selection) that I can deal with, the portion of the Book of Exodus called Ki Tisa, which includes the story of the Golden Calf. It's easy for me to see why the Jews got tired of waiting for Moses to come down from Mount Sinai and why they begged Aaron to create a false god out of their jewelry.

Patience is a virtue any 13-year-old can use. And it sure beats the portion assigned to the only other available Saturday, that known as Metzora, the story about an outbreak of leprosy.

While Samantha is happily looking ahead to her moment of triumph, I'm somewhat wobbly. Being a single mom planning a bat mitzvah is weird and, in my circle, unusual. I haven't yet faced the photographer or the video maker, for whom the creation of happy family icons is an art form. As for the deejay, I'm desperately searching for a way around the father-daughter dance.

At first I was so aware that Burton was missing that I couldn't move ahead even to pick a date. But now I've convinced myself that the ceremony is about a girl's acceptance of religious responsibility.

What a relief that the honor is hers alone.

While many of my friends are single, most of them got that way via divorce. For every friend who ever told me that having a dead husband is better than having a live ex, in preparation for their child's Jewish ritual, somehow dead husbands usually lose their clout.

It used to amaze me how, for the limited purpose of the bar and bat mitzvah, furiously estranged couples become endearingly reconciled.

"We're still a great team, you know," my friend Mel insists as he goes on about how he and Betty picked the caterer and chose the flowers. From my own admittedly jaundiced position, this touching display of family unity, for the sake of der kinde, always strikes me as somewhat suspect. I guess phony harmony beats open warfare, or the pain which occurs when one spouse has remarried and wants his new wife up on the bimah, sanctifying the relationship before the Torah scrolls. No wonder rabbis offer pre-bar mitzvah family counseling.

As I get closer to my own daughter's big day, I begin to see why having two parents is so crucial: One parent to plan the event, and the other to be the Designated Murder Victim.

The Designated Murder Victim (DMV) is the person whose job it is to catch all flak, to absorb all the tension, to be the one who doesn't do enough to lighten the load of the parent doing all the work. The necessity of the DMV should be obvious to anyone who has ever attended a smoothly running bar or bat mitzvah. Up on the dais, all looks peaceful and loving. But behind the scenes... the muffled sounds of the shotgun are evident.

In Hebrew school circles these days, there's lots of talk about "putting God on the guest list", a reminder that this is a life-cycle ritual we're planning and not a Sweet 16. Nevertheless, I'm less worried about the Almighty's appearance than who else might decide to show up. Many of my distant relatives find the idea of traveling cross country for a bat mitzvah the Jewish equivalent of jet-setting, and the guest list is exploding by the minute.

I'm not at the explosion stage myself, but the tension is mounting. This is predictable of course. Even growing up I knew that regularly scheduled blowups are a crucial part of fun family times. Which is why, having no one to yell at, I feel so nervous.

Can my daughter's bat mitzvah celebration be a success if I don't threaten to have a nervous breakdown once a week? Before my wedding, my mother threw a fit not at my father, who had opted out of his DMV status right after he hired the photographer for my brother's bar mitzvah 10 years before, but at me. She was irate, first that I ignored her entreaties to pick the menu and then, having picked the menu, that I wouldn't second guess the decision with her 20 more times. To be DMV at my own wedding was so memorable that I vowed my daughter will never do that role for me.

Nevertheless, there is a void I have tried to fill. I fell in love for a time with a man who seemed tailor made for flak-catching, having seen several other children through their own Jewish rituals. I tried enlisting my best friends for the job of soothsayer and second-guesser. I have contemplated, but rejected, feigning infatuation for my car repairman so I can have company on the dais.

Finally, I considered hiring a party planner. How perfect, a person whose job it is to be the object my frantic anxieties. Immediately after we met, the party planner began doing her job, calling me so incessantly with reminders about tasks to do and decisions that I alone could make that I instantly wanted to kill her. Trouble is, I have a reputation in this town and have to treat my help well. That I could not afford to get angry at the person I was hiring explicitly so there was someone I could get angry at made me mad.

We have three months left to go.

November, 1994

The Child Within

My daughter asks, "Mommy, were you anxious before your bat mitzvah?" We've entered the nerve-wracking period, only one month to go before Samantha's big day.

"I didn't have one," I answer.

"You didn't have a bat mitzvah?"

I'd been mentally preparing my answer for so long, you'd think I could just spit it out. I had never told her, not wanting to influence my daughter's own engaging experience. But ever since my twelfth birthday, I'd been nursing a grievance. When I was growing up, young girls had a second-rate ritual on Friday nights; my mother made it clear that my relatives would never take the three hour subway/railroad ride from Brooklyn to Long Island just to see a girl read a few Hebrew prayers and give a little speech in English. Worse, the rabbi made it clear that once I was 13, I couldn't sit up on the bimah and lead services as I had at junior congregation. I would be a woman, and women did not count.

"You see how bad it was!" I would tell her, and she would know she was standing before the scrolls not only for me, but on behalf of all women throughout time.

But of course that's not the way it works. After all, I loathed hearing my parents stories of the Depression. I looked into my daughter's eyes, so fully committed to her own coming of age, so naturally accepting of the freedoms that are hers without effort; my hoary history seemed incidental.

"Well, those were the days before women's equality," I explained.

"Pretty cheesy," she said.
"Yeah, it's a lot better now."

No child goes through a bar or bat mitzvah alone. Just ask the parents. Lilith magazine recently featured an interview with one Judy Davis, an expert in the field of psychology of bat and bar mitzvah. Dr. Davis calls it a "ritual ordeal." She notes, "Mother is being tested (by herself as well as by others) in her capacity as 'balabusta,' her capacity — in the most sacred sense of the word — as preparer of food, provider of comfort, and protector of harmony." What's at stake for Mom, she says, "is her capacity to protect [family] connections."

As for Dad, Davis says, he "embodies the sense of loss, the sense of the changing of the generational guards." If you, like me, are playing both mom and pop in this coming of age, you've got your hands full.

For today's parents, the passing on of Jewish life is thwart with ambivalence. Let us be candid: the connection with Judaism over the last 30-odd years has been tense, ambivalent, a long rocky ride. We've rebelled, criticized, embraced and repelled a Jewish world at once too large and too small for our own meager imaginings. Now we're back, "normal" Jews once more, intent on raising our children to a love of Torah. Do you think we can hide the impact of that roller coaster ride either from ourselves or the keen eye of our children? Don't bet on it.

Did your parents force you to have not only the bar mitzvah ceremony but the tedious party that went with it? Did the rabbi forget your name or treat you like a moron? Are you secretly thrilled that your son/daughter finds Hebrew school boring, confirming your own experience ages ago? Or, are you unnerved to find that your daughter or son not only loves the ritual but wants a gala event including the schmaltzy candle lighting ceremony to go with it?

Beware the "child within," your uninvited guest whose demands, like those of Rumpole's wife, must be obeyed.

Over the last five months, as Samantha sits in her room with her door closed, mastering Torah trope, little air bubbles of jealousy periodically boil up inside me. I have had to suppress the instinct to learn musical notation myself, and to demand that I read from the scrolls on her own landmark day. The competitive instinct is not unique to me: Several of my friends actually threatened to have a joint mother/daughter bat mitzvah, until they came to their senses. Even now I find myself yearning to research "Ki Tisa," Samantha's Torah portion, and to write my own devar Torah, an interpretation on the Golden Calf. What a job I could do on the role of Aaron in the creation of a molten idol.

A few weeks ago, when the urge to get in on her act was the most persistent, I became almost manic with concern that she hadn't learned anything at all during her 10 years at Hebrew nursery and religious school. One day, I broke out in a sweat imagining Samantha up there at the podium, not even knowing the "Shema."

"Don't you think you should study the prayers?" I asked her. "I mean, do you know the 'V'ahavta?'" "V'ahavta" is the basic b'nai mitzvah prayer, the second verse of the "Shema" and explains that the words of the Torah should be taught "diligently to your children."

To my shock, out it came, completely, perfectly memorized. I was happy to feel ashamed.

As she prepares, what Frost called the sweetness of bitter bark and burning clove overtakes me. My daughter will do what I did not. And my history can finally be left behind.

January, 1995

In the Details

When philosophers note that "God is in the details," they usually don't think about towel bars.

I'm writing this five days before Samantha's bat mitzvah. For me, there is still time to obsess, and I'm making the most of every minute.

Over the past six months, I have had my anxieties generally under control. Sure, I raised to an art form concern about Samantha's Torah portion, the restaurant for the post-service luncheon, the menu, the guest list, the invitations (I didn't order enough and had to spend much of a day at Kinko's redesigning an extra supply), the deejay and the clothes Samantha and I would wear for the occasion. But this was in the early stage, when every decision could be amended.

But now I'm in stage two of my anxiety, and we're getting down, as we used to say, to the real nitty-gritty: MY FAMILY IS COMING!!!! It's not that they don't visit periodically, but not all at once. My parents, my brother Alan and his friend Tom and cousin Lorraine and her daughter Brittany will be staying with us or nearby. And like any Jewish woman on the eve of a big family occasion, I am embarrassed.

When I was growing up and company was coming, my mother would run around the house, dashing up and down stairs, darting into the corners, digging behind lamps and chairs.

"Dust!" she said. Or, "Lint!" I saw nothing, but then what did I know.

"Do you want to embarrass me?" my mother said. "Take out the vacuum. And this time, wear your glasses." There was nothing in the corners, but like the search for chametz (the crumbs of bread and forbidden food) at Passover, I suspect she put some there, just to make herself feel better.

And now it is my turn. Standards of domestic cleanliness have declined since I was a child, thanks to the woman's movement, but the feelings of accountability to society still remain. Normally, I do a lot of looking away: The things I refuse to see that need repairing would fill a filing cabinet. Whole months go by when I don't look at my house with the kind of clear-eyed once-over my mother offered her home every weekend.

Usually I'm O.K. with this, but then my mother comes to visit, and suddenly my vision turns 20-20. There have been moments lately when, running around the house, darting into the corners, digging behind lamps and chairs, I've felt like taking a match to the whole thing. How can I let people see how I live!

And so my anxieties have focused around my towels and my towel bar, or rather lack of same. Since I painted the bathroom about a year ago, I never replaced the towel bar, so loosely engaged on the wall the bar would slip into the tub with an ugly clank that shook the china cabinet next door. You think this is stupid stuff, don't you! But in the last two weeks every bit of my self-image as a stable parent raising a child has focused here. The ripped towels hanging on the glass shower door haven't helped either. Is this the way my mother raised me? I'd say not.

And so, as my deadline approaches I have day after day visited every hardware and department store in Los Angeles. I feel foolish, and yet this preparatory anxiety is normal, or at least everyone I know has had it. Before their daughter's bat mitzvah, my friends Stan and Eleanor put a whole second story on their house. Paul and Phyllis completely gutted their kitchen and made a built-in marble table top. My friend Jamie redid her driveway in brick.

This anxiety, oddly enough, fits the occasion. This is where critics of Jewish life have it wrong. They think that parental obsession with the party, the food, the flowers and the music is a rejection of the Jewish religious spirit of the day, an example of Jewish sumptuary extravagance, a reversion to old bourgeois habits of showing off wealth.

Nothing doing. Perversely, parents become concerned with these frivolous externals because of the spiritual nature of what's going on around them, their child is coming of age.

The more Samantha worries about her Hebrew and her speech, the more I see how little I can help her. I haven't felt so powerless since the day she started kindergarten. What can I do to help my girl?! Nothing. If only I could stand up there behind her and pull strings like a puppeteer! But there's nothing I can do, and increasingly little left I can constructively worry about.

No use worrying now about the deejay. We spoke for the first time last night. To my horror, he's never heard of klezmer music, and seems to think that all Jewish music is the hora. He did know, however, everyone of Samantha's favorite hip-hop groups and has every one of the Salt-n-Pepa discs. And he's actually done me a favor, finding a good klezmer disc to bring with me has given me something new to obsess about.

Because as these things happen, my towel problem finally ended. Whatever I saved by making my own centerpieces has now gone into Egyptian cotton bath sheets. And after buying and returning five towel bars, I put my old clanky one back on the wall.

Still, I'm a realist: Something will go wrong. My seating chart may be a mess. Or — horrors — the deejay may play the wrong song at Samantha's grand entrance. A lawsuit about just such a thing was in small claims court just last week.

When it comes to things to worry about, towels seem safe.

February, 1995

The Great Day

At Kehillat Israel synagogue in Pacific Palisades, the bar- and bat mitzvah ritual contains an epiphanic moment: the Ark is opened and the sacred Torah scrolls, dressed in velvet robe and adorned with silver crown and shields, is physically passed from grandparents to parents and then to the child in his or her thirteenth year.

"Don't worry," the rabbi told my father and mother last Saturday. "You'll be holding the Torah but I'll be there right behind you."

I have watched this ritual many times and it never fails to stir me, to twist up my innards and make physical what is so often in my head.

The Torah is much more than the Five Books of Moses, with printed words and paper pages. It is an ancient scroll containing our history and our law, written with turkey feather quill on animal hide in an ink of gall-nuts, gum arabic and copper sulfate crystals.

The sheets of parchment are tied together with thread made of tendon tissue taken from the foot muscles of a kosher animal. When the scroll is wound up and dressed, 10,416 lines of Hebrew calligraphy are encased in a 20-pound body about 3 1/2 feet tall, with two legs, a wobbly "head" and a soft, almost seductive, middle, encouraging embrace. For one who is drawn near to the Torah, the human size and dimension are impossible to dismiss, provoking at once both awe at its longevity and tender parental concern for its protection. One thing for sure: here is not a museum relic, a dusty symbol or a dry icon, but a living testament to an undying faith, and we are part of it. The Torah is incapable of standing alone, but needs a wooden stand, or a man or a woman, to hold it erect.

First my father took the Torah, then my mother, then me. And finally it was Samantha's turn. She looked, for a moment, so young and vulnerable, with the Torah leaning high on her right shoulder, it was as if she was holding her favorite bear. Then she straightened herself up, set a smile on her face, and with bells and silver jangling, went out among the people.

"For out of Zion came the Torah," sang the standing congregation. People charged up to us, crowding around on all sides, holding out their prayer shawls and prayer books to kiss first the velvet dress and then their lips. We walked slowly in a circle, my family formed an army, a brigade, an honor guard, led by a child. Then we once again mounted the dais and everyone was seated. It was time for the Law to be read.

Every culture has its rite of passage, its moment of entry and requirements of adult behavior. In America, throwing a ball across a 30 yard line, or finding a career goal is what it takes to belong. For young Jews, reading words off animal skin provides a trial of a different but not lesser kind. The bar/bat mitzvah accomplishes precisely what anthropologist Barbara Myerhoff once insisted such a ritual must: providing a great moment of spiritual transformation strong enough to carry an adolescent across the chasm of chaos and fear.

It's no easy thing, reading from the Torah scroll. It contains about 312,480 letters; 248 columns of 42 lines each. Each column is 30 letters wide, in an intricate Hebrew lettering full of flourishes and adornments. There is no punctuation, no vowels, commas, periods or colons. You either know what you're reading or you don't. Moreover, the Torah scroll must be sung, never merely read aloud, for the words of the Teachings bring delight to the ear and the soul.

Samantha took the yad, the silver pointer in the shape of a hand, and prepared to read. Surrounding her were the cantor and her grandparents, who had just read the introductory blessings for the Torah reading.

My mother, enveloped in my father's prayer shawl, was called to the Torah in her own Hebrew name and was finally close enough to see the inscribed words.

Samantha's hair was in a French twist. Her new blue and white tallit was on her shoulders. She looked older and younger than ever before. Seated before her was everyone who believed in her, loved her and cared that she succeed in this world.

"Maxwell, Michelle, Zack, Abby and Marla all did it. And now it's my turn," she would say as kind of a mantra of preparation. In the order of things, being bat mitzvah was as natural and expected to her as getting a driver's license or going to college. And here it was, the moment for which she had been preparing for many years, doing precisely what was hers to do.

"*Va-yidabair Adonoi el Moshe lai'mor: Ki Tisa...*" she chanted. "And God said to Moses, count the people..." She sang out so strong, anyone could see: this was not a recitation of a memorized script, but a metaphysical hook-up, a young woman making contact with a world, a people, a history, a text.

Later,we were sitting on the dais, Samantha and I on either side of the ark. The room was full, the ceremony half done. She turned to me.

"Mommy," she whispered, her voice with great seriousness and greater joy. "This is so wonderful!"

It certainly is.

February, 1995

Yeast is Yeast

I don't know where my fascination for baking challah comes from, or even why. My mother never baked bread. I think that, like me, she may be awed by yeast, or distressed by failure. At any rate, challah was not her thing, and yet somehow it has come to be mine.

Over the years I have experimented with more eggs and fewer, with doubling the yeast, with adding more sugar and less. I have used wooden bowls for proofing and metal bowls and flours, wheat, rye, unbleached. Today I rise to tell you that the answer is in none of these. The answer to challah is time.

On one level challah is just high-level bread, yeasty, golden-brown, architecturally profound with its high dome and Gaudi-esque curls. But of course it is much more. Challah is a commandment, one of only three out of the total 613 that are the special province of women (the others being lighting candles and the ritual bath). Without challah on the table you can't have a Friday night meal and without the Friday night meal, the Sabbath cannot begin. So making challah is like setting the stage for a historic psychodrama, helping to move the Jewish people on its way from work to rest.

Everything about the bread is symbolic. The curls which result from the braiding of three long ropes of dough represent God, Torah and the people of Israel, the three legs of Jewish life. The crested shape represents the prayers of Jews ascending to heaven. (In California, we sometimes make the six-legged version, on the theory that it is twice as holy.)

Its ingredients, ample, extravagant, calling for upwards of four eggs, makes of us all, for a night, Tevye's "rich man." It's terrific to note that in the current rage for gourmet bread buying, a luxuriant challah, shiny crusted, laced with raisins or poppy seeds or even, incredibly, chocolate chips, has finally superseded the traditional Jewish bread of choice, the European rye. Challah has been restored to its regency.

Even the sages knew that a home-made challah is not easy, and implicitly dangerous for the novice. A novice is in a rush, placing product and perfection ahead of the soul. That's why the Talmud distinguishes between producing the challah, that is, insuring that two loaves are on the table each Shabbat (the second symbolizes the extra portion of manna delivered each Friday during the wandering in the desert) and making the loaves themselves. If a household can afford the services of a cook (or implicitly if a non-baking husband makes it or the family buys one at the bakery) that's fine too. What is being acknowledged here is the spiritual nature of sustenance and that when challah fails — turning out tough, or ugly, or flat and lopsided with air holes — it is an epic disaster, an affront to the angels of good taste.

And the angels do have something to do with it. In their book, *Four Centuries of Jewish Women's Spirituality*, editors Ellen M. Umansky and Dianne Ashton reprint several ancient *tkhines*, a form of personal prayer popular among women. One of them, entitled "On Putting the Sabbath Loaf into the Oven," dating back at least to 1648 Amsterdam, suggests just how much is felt to be at stake even after the challah dough has been mixed and kneaded and left to rise, then punched down and shaped and left to rise again.

"Send an angel to guard the baking," the *tkhine* pleads, "so that all will be well baked, will rise nicely, and will not burn, to honor the holy Sabbath (which you have chosen so that Israel your children may rest thereon) and over which one recites the holy blessing — as you blessed the dough of Sarah and Rebecca our mothers." Please Almighty One, let this experiment succeed.

I love making challah. I like the way it mixes the holy with the mundane. I like the way the dough, elastic but not too wet, reminds me of a powdered baby's bottom. I like the way that kneading the dough, incorporating flour and air with the heel of my hand, bending my body into the belly of the ball, always reminds me of sex. I like shaping the mound and punching down into its womb, and the dark oaky smell ripe with leaven and hope. I like watching the air holes emerge in the braiding process, a peek at the universe within. During the eight days of Passover, when Jews stop eating leavened bread, it's the lack of making challah that seems the great deprivation. During that whole week I am forced to consider the misery of plain life without yeast, and it seems a meager prospect indeed. Compared with the inflated loaves of challah, matzoh is indeed the bread of affliction. As these things go, making even a bad challah is a more acceptable expenditure of time than, say, perfecting my pizza crust. And with pizza you can't make a terrific French toast the next day.

That's where the matter of time comes in. If there's a reason so many of my early challahs have come to disaster, it is perhaps that I was young. I believed the cookbooks, which stressed economy and efficiency and how easy it all could be. In the bad challahs I have made, the goal, my *kavannah* or spiritual intention, was merely the product; no angels need apply.

But over time I have learned. That some things are known but cannot be explained. Some senses felt, but not described. Love, of course. Injustice. And when dough has had sufficient time to rise.

If you give it time, making challah is easy. You need

time to develop your own style, your own knowledge of who you are, bread-baking-wise. Once, I joined a group of women in Kiev as we tried to bring Yiddishkeit to the Jews of the former Soviet Union. These were Eastern European women who had gone 50 years without Jewish ritual or tradition, and they took to it eagerly.

On the Friday morning before Shabbat, two of the Americans got the bright idea of offering a challah-baking demonstration. They inspected the kitchen, they negotiated with the chefs, they went hunting for ingredients throughout the markets of Kiev. They were so excited at the forthcoming demonstration, like they were presenting a dowry to a bride.

But as the planning went on, the American women could agree on nothing, not the number of eggs, not the amount of water, not how to knead the dough. I swear there was almost a fist-fight in the kitchen. "You have to dance with the challah, like a lover," said one. "You have to prod it gently, like a baby," said the other.

I use attorney Sabrina Schiller's "best challah" recipe which is basically seven cups of flour to four eggs. I start early Friday morning (in some houses it starts Thursday night.)

Sabrina Schiller's Best Challah Ever

2 cakes yeast
1 3/4 cups lukewarm water
1 tablespoons salt
1/2 cup sugar
1/4 cup (1/2 stick) butter or margarine
7 cups flour (and a little more)
4 large eggs (beaten — can use Eggbeaters)
sesame seeds and/or poppy seeds

Dissolve the yeast in the water. Add the salt, sugar, and beaten eggs. Add the melted, cooled butter or margarine. Blend in 4 cups of the flour, then beat, either with an electric mixer or 400 times by hand, until the mixture is smooth. And 3 more cups flour and stir in.

Turn out onto a floured board or counter, and knead until smooth and elastic. Re-flour breadboard as necessary to keep dough from sticking as you knead, being careful not to use too much. (To knead, press down on the lump of dough with your two palms, fold the bread over on itself from back to front, turn clockwise, then repeat the procedure — press-fold-turn.)

Place in buttered bowl, cover with a clean cloth, and let rise until doubled. Punch the dough down and turn it out again on a lightly floured breadboard. Braid. Let rise until doubled. Bake in oven at 350° for 45 minutes. Loaves are done when tapping on top yields a hollow sound. The angels have arrived.

March, 1995

Getting Schmaltzy

Chicken fat! There, I said it.

Are there two words more prone to elicit Jewish guilt? Go ahead, repeat them out loud: Chicken fat! I know what you're thinking: Liquid cholesterol. Death in a teaspoon. Murder most fowl.

If bagels and lox is Jewish-America's essential dish, chicken fat is its scoundrel, beloved in memory, but by now outlawed by popular consensus, consigned to be a relic, like snuff. We modern Jews have become like Jack Sprat without a wife, eating not only no fat, but no meat, no dairy, no fish, no lactose. Our contemporary fetish with a minimalist palate of pasta, pasta, pasta shows its dark side during the week of Passover, when noodles and bread are forbidden by Jewish law. Maybe we will live the proverbial 120 years, maybe it's our boring diet that will make it feel that way. Just last week at the seder table, a friend who is vegetarian said that she wished she didn't care about food at all. Sure, I say, and let's not care about music, or art, or sex as well. The very question my father used to ask rhetorically, do you live to eat or eat to live, is no question at all.

My friends, I will admit it to you. Last week, I cooked with chicken fat. I made a tsimmes (more about this in a minute) and used schmaltz to sauté onions and potatoes. Go ahead, shoot me. I was just sick of saying no. I have been to Paris. I have eaten a dinner of chocolate truffles. I have satisfied all manner of earthly cravings. But using less than a quarter cup of chicken fat to season a pound of beef, two cups of onions, two pounds of carrots and a 3 pounds of potatoes in the making of a tsimmes, — this, and this alone, I had never, until now, seen fit to indulge.

I had secretly yearned for this for some time. Last year I went so far as to actually pick up a bottle of chicken fat at the matzoh section of my market. Solid fat at the base, a golden yellow emulsion at the top. The voices of all my dead relatives shouted out at me, "Who are you kidding!" I tossed it back like an underweight fish.

But we only live once, right? This is the end of the 20th century, and we must each wage our war against political correctness. There is chicken fat in our history, and it's time to face it squarely. So I brought home the bottle and sat it next to the oven. I looked at the chicken fat, asking: How many Jews have died on your behalf? But what had been the alternative? It wasn't as if the world of the ghetto had 95 types of oleo and margarine. (Butter, of course, could not be used for meat.) Until the invention of Crisco in 1910, Jewish homes had no alternative to chicken fat except imported (hence expensive) olive oil. Chicken fat made in our own kitchens, grease splattering from the renderings and a bottle of schmaltz ready for the rye bread, gave the Jewish home its smell and, in hindsight, its feel.

In 1910, harassed Jewish parents, sick of hand-made oil, rushed to embrace the new invention Crisco as the product "the Hebrew Race had been waiting 4,000 years" as Procter & Gamble advertised. (My mother never touched the stuff, it still seemed unJewish to her.) Even now, 85 years later, it's for chicken fat we still mourn.

Now a word about tsimmes. Not for nothing has tsimmes entered the American vernacular as "a big fuss." Coming from the German *zum essen*, "to eat," a tsimmes takes hours to make and everything about it is a matter of debate: Like a Cezanne still life, everything must be in proportion. How much meat, the size of the sweet potatoes, do you use uniform carrots (I use a bag of miniatures) how many prunes and when to add them? Once you start there's no going back, since cooking takes almost 3 hours.

Given all the controversy, chicken fat added to tsimmes is not exactly the major battle of the war. I could have used vegetable oil and probably no one but me would have known the difference.

My recipe is based on one from Joan Nathan's marvelous *Jewish Cooking in America*, winner of the Julia Child award for best cookbook.

Joan Nathan's Tzimmes

Brown 3 pounds beef flanken or short ribs (salt and pepper to taste) with 3 medium sliced onions in 2 tablespoons of chicken fat or oil. Place the meat and onions in a casserole and cover it with 6 cups water or beef bouillon, cook for 2 hours. Cut 3 large, peeled sweet potatoes then add 5 large peeled carrots, 3 peeled large white potatoes, 3/4 pounds each of dried pitted prunes and dried apricots, 1/4 cup brown sugar, 1/4 cup apricot jam, dash nutmeg, 1/2 teaspoon cinnamon, juice of one lemon, slivered rind and juice of 1 orange. Add to meat mixture. Set in 350 degree oven for 90 minutes.

For potato topping, mix 1 large peeled and grated white potato with 2 cups matzoh meal, 2 eggs, 2 tablespoons fresh parsley, 1 onion, coarsely grated; 1 tablespoon chicken fat (this is where I used it) or oil, and salt and pepper to taste. Add up to 1/2 cup water to make a sticky dough. Flouring your hands, spread the potato dough and press very thinly over the tsimmes and bake, covered for 45 minutes more.

Uncover, season with salt and pepper, and cook until the top turns crusty. Delicious!

April, 1995

Part Four
More than a Single Life

"When the heart is full,

the eyes overflow"

Yiddish proverb

Whole New World

When my parents announced that they wanted to sell their home in Plainview, New York, I thought, "OK, I'll buy it myself."

It was preposterous, of course. I'd been living in a home of my own in Los Angeles for twenty years, far longer than the seven I'd spent on Long Island. My L.A. years, corresponding to my marriage, motherhood, career, widowhood and a bank of eucalyptus trees now forty feet tall, have been far more crucial to my own becoming than the anguished nether world of adolescence spent in suburbia.

Plus, I'd always hated Plainview when I lived there, so far from the city and a life of healthy idiosyncrasy that a neighbor called my parents when she saw me necking with a boyfriend in the local movie theater.

Nevertheless, the reflex was natural and true. Something in me was planted in the Plainview top soil; I was a Long Island girl, with a Long Islander's sense of America, a feeling of expandable destiny.

One Sunday when I was about twelve, we stood in a downpour under the tar paper roof and two-by-fours that constituted what was soon to be Minnie Weinstock's house on Phipps Lane. Gazing out the open framed window, there were potato fields as far as the eyes could see. The flat unbounded land, close enough to good schools, a shopping center and an expressway exit to assure that civilization was yet at hand, was thrilling to my folks who had lived all their lives with shared bathrooms and angry neighbors dictating what time was too late to take a shower.

My father looked at my mother there on Phipps Lane as if the two of them were part of the Lewis & Clark expedition when it finally reached the Pacific coast. Home, they said. This is home.

Now, even as Mom and Dad went about their business of finding a buyer, opening escrow and locating an apartment closer to Manhattan, I kept up the fantasy of buying the house from them. What was I saying here, that the frontier which had been L.A. was closing in? That there was no way to go but back?

No, I was recalibrating what it means to be free.

I imagined Samantha living in my brother's old room with the wood shutters hand-made by my father; I would take up the master suite with the adjoining bathroom and shower. Samantha would go to a junior high I never attended but we would join the same synagogue and shop at the local Food Town with the massive deli section that stocked four kinds of chopped herring.

My daughter would be happy there, since nothing worse could happen to her than happened to me: her seventh grade class would be plagued only by the 1990s equivalent of Jane Glatz, whose father was a psychologist and who looked at every friend as if she were a case study of neurosis. Or Linda Wolf whose father ran a dentist's office out of their home and whose opinions on movies and music came right out of Time magazine. Or Sharon Solomon, whose mother spent her days washing towels and scrubbing floors until Sharon's father came home, put Sinatra on the turntable and sent the children to their rooms. The social density of my youth, which once approximated *Carrie* in its ambition and viciousness, seems now only predictably competitive and narrowly sociopathic. A happy place to be.

By buying our home in Plainview, Samantha and I would become one more family, one more anonymous light under the portico, amid acres and miles of similar lights, a family restored to the sanity of conformity. For the moment it gave me insupportable pleasure.

"The Thads love this house," my mother was saying. A young couple with two school-age children had discovered the house last Halloween and had quite begged my parents to sell it to them. "They want us out of here before September," said Mom.

I missed my chance. Perhaps I never wanted to move in, but only that they should stay.

"Can you imagine some other family living here?" my mother asks. Well, yes. But what I can't imagine is us not being there ourselves. So long as my parents stayed put in the old split level, time stood still. I went back each year, Plainview's sameness and predictability casting a comforting shadow on my life's own turbulence. It was a lie of continuity that made me feel whole.

Maybe every generation thinks of itself as pioneers. From the flat open land my parents' era tended has emerged: the schools, the temple, the bakery, the bowling alley, the local beauty parlor and the Italian restaurant which serves pizza with five kinds of crust. There are huge green maples outside the front door which turn amber and gold each fall; cherry blossoms burst lacy and pink each spring.

The packing up process has begun. Thirty-two years boiled down to fourteen boxes of books, seventeen types of screwdrivers, a wall full of hats from foreign places.

"Better we should do this together now than that you and Alan should do it alone later," my mother says.

In the garage sale, my mother sold my grandmother's old trundle sewing machine, my father's extra tools, my brother's bedroom set.

"Do you want the wall map?" my father asked about the projection chart that had been in Alan's room

since his bar mitzvah.
"A map of 1965?" I said.
"How about the wood globe? Can Samantha use it?"
"It's a whole new world now," I said.
He answered, "Thanks a lot for reminding me."

October, 1994

What Me Worry?

"Are you studying?"
"Did you give Lindsay the book?"
"Put the light on. You can't read in the dark."
"That blouse is too skimpy."
"You've been on the phone an hour!"

"The milk glass has been in the living room for a week. Please! pick up it up."

As a mother, I'm a real pain in the butt, but here's the shocker: I nag on purpose. Yes, every so often, when the house is too quiet, I'll wander around, looking for something to bray about. I'll poke my head into my daughter's room, like a detective with a flashlight, coming upon her while she's gazing at herself in the mirror fantasizing about some great guy at school; or reading her YM magazine or better yet, I'll catch her right in the middle of her favorite show, *Models Inc.*

"Is your homework done yet?" I'll say benignly. "Good, then how about cleaning up your room." Or, "How about reading a book?" Or, on the weekend I'll pull out my very favorite accusation, a family heirloom, "It's a beautiful day, go for a walk. How can you bear to be inside?" True, I've ruined her perfectly peaceful solitude, but I feel better.

If nudging was God's second communication with Adam ("Be fruitful and multiply,") then outright nagging was the second: "Don't eat the apple!" It's a biologically predetermined instinct, a way of building in conscience and reminding us that we are not alone, that others are watching. As my mother used to say, "If I didn't criticize you, how would you know I care?"

How indeed. Today's family experts suggest that children learn more by example than by lecture, but you can never be sure.

Anyway, worrying is not for the benefit of the child, but for the relief of the parent, a pressure value on normal anxiety.

As a mother, there's always something to worry about, real or imagined. Whether or not I nag my daughter about it depends upon how much a worry nags (that is, nibbles or gnaws) at me. Most of my maternal worries are beyond my control; mere nagging would be useless.

When Samantha was newborn, our visiting nurse criticized the way her belly button was healing: I took to my bed at once (it's fine, thank you.) Then, when she was about 18 months old I took her food shopping and left her in the grocery cart while I dashed around the corner for diapers. Instantly I had a panic attack, imagining that the floor of the market had opened up and swallowed her into it. I began to grieve at how the universe would feel with her gone, and that everything wonderful in my life would go with her.

Compared with those early those moments of cosmic anxiety, my present concerns seem relatively manageable, hence worth nagging about: Will she develop ambition and drive, a strong personal ethic and stable friendships, a love of literature, a sense of order? These are not small, or petty, but compared to the ground opening up, they come as a minor relief.

When I was a 15, my parents said I was too young to go out with a senior who called himself, even then, "S. Leonard Stein." I was appalled by their ruling and, deeply influenced by our class study of the French Revolution, I spent a whole teary afternoon writing in my diary about the uneven distribution of power between parents and children. "A family is like an oligarchy in which children have no advocates," I wrote pretentiously, "but inevitably it, like Louis XIV, will fall."

The modern family has indeed fallen on hard times, which is why it comes as a surprise to find that Mother's Day has now been inflated into a day of near-religious observance. Several of my friends, their mothers now dead, confided that they go into hiding on Mother's Day, and one even leaves town.

The fact is that friends may be concerned for you, and relatives are there in a pinch, but it's only a mother's operatic worry that counts. Obsessive, invasive, irrational, a mother's worry (whether communicated by silence or soliloquy) is a sign that the universe cares for us in a big way. And when she's gone, we find out too late there's nothing like it.

My mother, self-elected President of the Worry Club, stayed up until I came home from an evening out, even when I was in college. It drove me crazy, to round the bend to our street and catch the piercing glare of the front porch light, as if my mother's watchful gaze had been imprinted onto the bulb. What did she think would happen to me?

What she thought might happen to me worried her less than what she couldn't imagine. She operated from an article of faith: The safer the world appears, the more devastating is the horror to come. Something awful will happen to my child, she'll meet bad people, make bad friends, see bad movies, make bad judgments. Evil lurks everywhere, the snake in the garden. And when this beautiful love is gone, Paradise will be lost.

So I waited a long time to have a child, until arbitrary power no longer interested me. I would do it right, trusting myself, my child and the world. Worry would be unnecessary. Hah!

Just as soon as I got my worry for my daughter under control, a new wrinkle occurred: I began to worry about my parents.

My mother and father no longer leave the light on for me, but I find myself staying up late, worrying about them.

I worry when they call too often, or not enough. And, surprise, surprise, because in our house criticism is a form of compliment, I've begun to nag at them, too: "What did the doctor say?" "Do you need a second opinion?" "Are you watching your diet?" And from time to time I drag out my old favorite, "It's a beautiful day, go for a walk. How can you bear to be inside?"

May, 1995

Sandwich Generation

Mah nishtanah ha lilah ha zeh? Why is this night different?

When I took on the task of doing the seder well over a decade ago, it was with a nonchalance that veered toward contempt. Like Judy Garland and Mickey Rooney bursting out "Let's put on a show!" my idea of a seder was something of a lark. What could there be to it?

Hah! Let's not even consider the food, the wine, the seder plate or the logistics of seating 25-plus guests around a table for eight nor the problem of which *haggadah* to use to tell the story of the liberation from Egypt!

The real problem, unforeseen when the children were small, was how to handle their questions. My friends and I have smart kids, and over the years I have gotten by only with a little fancy footwork. Already their questions have veered into the challenging matter of why the Israelites were saved while the innocent Egyptian firstborn were killed. Who knows, maybe next Wednesday some wise-guy will make the equation between those sacrificed Egyptian sons of ancient history and the guiltless Palestinians who today are barred from working in a terrorized Israel, which is now building a fence between itself and the Palestinian Authority. Teenagers have a knack of asking disturbing questions and I, though eager to insist upon Israel's right to protect itself against suicide bombings, will have to know my stuff.

But I must admit that even as the show goes on, even as I break the third matzoh, the flat bread symbolizing affliction and define the purpose of the shank bone and the bitter herbs (respectively, sacrifice and slavery), my thoughts this year are elsewhere. I'm concerned this Passover not with why this night is different, but why it is the same.

It is the same because once again my parents will be at my seder table. For me, this year's Passover metaphor is Hillel's sandwich, the bitter herbs of mortality mixed in with the sweet charoset of time going by.

Should I admit the obvious? My friends and I have reached that stage when the older generation is an endangered species. More precious than rubies is a seder table with three intact generations: grandparents, parents and children. This year several in my circle lost not one parent but two, father following mother, or mother rapidly following father. We speak to each other these days in the language of loss. It is not strange to hear grown men and women in their forties assert that they are feeling like orphaned children.

I have invited to this year's Passover seder not only my own parents, but those of all my friends. Compassion and yearning fill my table to overflowing. I, who only years ago wanted only to be around people my age, to relish in the free lives we were creating forourselves, have come lately to enjoy the warmth and comfort that being around elders can bring. Who will tell the story of Depression and the New Deal? Who recalls the great American .labor movement? Who remembers FDR and Harry Truman and knows the truth about the downfall of Communism, about the Cold War and Vietnam?

The past is leaking away, and I am gathering it up, as if in coffee spoons. The way that I learned history — through the memories of my uncles and aunts — that's what I want for our children too.

Every new generation labels their elders as has-beens; but there's been nothing quite like us Boomers, tagging all who went before as chronically [ban that word!] dysfunctional. How smart we pretended to be. And how cruel.

"You want to make life easy for yourself?" my mother asks from Florida. "Why not serve a ready-made brisket?" My parents are older now, with nothing to prove. As a result, they expect less of me as well. If I decided to serve the entire seder meal on paper plates and plastic forks, they wouldn't bat an eye.

"You're making gefilte fish?" my mother asks, as if it strained credulity. She's got a short-cut for that, too, if I so desire: take a good quality gefilte fish from a jar and steam it in fresh fish stock so it tastes home made.

"You're sure you want to do seder both nights?" asks my father. "If we only had seder one night, *dayenu.*"

It's my parents who are asking the really compelling questions, this seder night, the questions of efficiency based on the enlightenment of years. It's not that they are frail; in fact both of them haven't felt so well in years. It's just that now in their seventies, they know what's worth the effort, and what is a waste of precious time.

Why kill yourself over a meal? they want to know. Why not relax a little? Stop a while, enjoy yourself. What are you working so hard for? And about these questions, I still have so much to learn.

April, 1996

Mother Love

The eighth grade left for Washington last week and had to be at school by 5:45 A.M. for a 6:15 departure. Half way there, Samantha let out a gasp.

"I forgot my report!" she said. "The teacher will kill me."

Samantha had worked diligently on her report about the Smithsonian Institute's National Museum of Natural History, with its exhibits of a living coral reef, the Hope Diamond and a live insect zoo. She was expected to stand and deliver it immediately before her classmates entered the building.

Mortified at her own forgetfulness, she was cursing herself silently. Looking at the clock, I considered her plight. The sane part of me whispered, "It's her problem. Let her pay the price." But sanity was quickly overruled by a passion that was hard to name Was it love? Empathy? Or simply the desire to avoid shame? The sweat of my own childhood bouts of imperfection rose spontaneously to the surface, all the more unbearable because it was not me but my own child who was suffering unease. We were two separate beings locked into a singular quandary: What to do?

It was now 5:45 — just enough time for me to drop her off, turn around, retrieve the report from home and still get back before the bus left.

And so I did, retracing the 30 miles in the near dark, at risk of being tracked by police radar. When I arrived at the school, the sun was up and the bus was gone. How far could it have traveled? I raced down Mulholland Highway toward the 101 Freeway. Surely, the bus had left only minutes ago. Isn't that it, up ahead?

I got on the Ventura Freeway, heading toward the city; still no bus. Now I was stuck in traffic; there was nothing to do but keep on going.

The science report burned a hole in my being that only handing it to Samantha could chill. "You are the adult!" I said. "Grab hold of yourself!"

But I couldn't. As I drove east, past the White Oak exit, the nexus of my concern changed. Staring into the abyss of an incomplete homework assignment, I was suddenly launched into an orbit where parental anxieties are fueled by vestigial childhood fears.

When I was about 8, my family went for a week to a country retreat so that my mother might recuperate from a hospitalization. I liked to swim in the lake, but one day I went out too far into the deep.

Gasping for air, I bobbed up and down in the water, trying to dog paddle, but I kept touching the muddy bottom. Flailing about, I saw my mother running desperately into the water, her paisley skirt and white blouse billowing like sails. She moved toward me in slow motion, her face a sine wave of concern. Hours after I was safely dry, all she could say was, "I didn't even have time to take off my peds."

There is a love that is blind to cause and effect, that has no concern with effort, result or reason. This is mother love, even when a father enacts it. Love so close to the essence, so based on survival, it expresses all danger as life or death, flight or fight — all, but never nothing at all.

A woman sacrifices her stockings for a child. We do not question why. But what about the smaller crises? Try as I might, as a mother, I fight a continual battle with moderation. I ask myself the right questions, such as "whose battle is this?" and "why is solving this problem up to you?" But sometimes, psychotherapists be damned, danger veers up like Satan, an apparition that only I can see, and whose potential malevolence I can't ignore.

A friend of mine remembers calling her parents from her new dorm the first September she went off to college. After hearing about her roommates, class schedule and her new, independent life, her mother signed off by saying, "Don't slip on the leaves."

The parenting instinct is inherently one without a sense of proportion. For our children, nature is never neutral; even the fallen leaves hold the seeds of disaster. And age provides no buffer to security. Recently, after I returned from a trip to Asia, my mother breathed audibly in relief.

"I couldn't wait until you were home," she said.

It begins early, of course, this contest with the demons, A missing ribbon from a costume for the class play, a lost catcher's mitt or a piece of music wrongly copied for the violin concert — tiny mishaps throw the parent's world off course. Out onto the brink we go, sacrificing not only our stockings but our sanity, to set things right. How could it be otherwise: For to be a parent is to be out of control, to watch power shift gradually away from ourselves onto the new generation. We live in a universe where things usually go wrong, maybe in order that the growing child can, by wit and cunning, learn to resolve crises herself.

As I transported the natural history report down the road, my universe was in shambles. Samantha not only lacked her Smithsonian report and the bottled water we'd bought at the all-night market at 4:30 A.M., but we hadn't said good-bye!

This really killed me. How could I let her go off for five days without a kiss from her mommy?

I was insane, feeling more out of control by the

moment. But I couldn't help myself. By now, I'd left the Ventura Freeway and was passing the Wilshire Boulevard exit down the southbound 405. Might as well go to the airport, I said to myself. If I don't see this kid, I'm lost.

I got to the gate, happy in my own crazy way. I hugged my daughter and felt the world restored to harmony.

"Mommy, you came!" she said, gaily. And then she added, as I feared she would, "You know, my teacher said you could have faxed the report to me."

May, 1996

Remember My Name

Samantha came home from nearly four weeks at Camp Hess Kramer and has begun calling me "Eema." Her voice, as she evokes the Hebrew word for mother is so intimate, so lovingly natural that I feel a kind of benign safety in my own home. With a teenager there's no telling how it will go. Sometimes we're on the same track, the two of us happily tooling along to Tori Amos on the car radio. And then, bang! We'll collide over Nirvana, domestic peace blown to smithereens.

When I was Samantha's age, 14 1/2, I stopped using the word "Mommy," against the more formal "Mother." It made me feel older, wiser, immune from childish stupidity; as if by changing one word I could pass into adulthood, with my own car and my own life. Mother. I still see her cheek pinched in pain at the affront. A few months later I tried calling her Anne. "Did you go to school with me?" she asked rhetorically. How corrosive is youth, one day we're trying out Mom's shade of blush, the next day blotting her out entirely.

"I'll always be your mother, I'll never be your friend," my mother used to tell me. She felt that establishing distance would instill respect. But in a single-parent family, friendship goes with the territory; harmony in the household depends upon the child's good will. From the beginning, Samantha has had to make excuses for me, understand my moods, move herself into the rhythm of my week. Evan Kleiman, the chef/owner of the Los Angeles restaurant Angeli, once told me that she learned to cook as a way of making sure that her single working mother had something to eat. That's friendship.

I no longer mind that Samantha can see the unvarnished, stressed-out me. Though the Torah says, "do not uncover the nakedness of thy father," I think it means, don't purposely look for flaws. Trying to be both dad and mom, the tiny curtain of parental infallibility does not fully cover me. Samantha stands with me underneath the drapery of my authority; she knows too well that like the Great Oz, there is no Great Mom, only a smoke machine, some mirrors and an earnest woman trying to get her life to work.

Being "Eema" seems precisely right for where I am now: located on my daughter's parental axis midway between total embrace and a stop-off just to change clothes. Sometimes I feel she is done with me completely, that my glory days of control and value are completely gone. I listen to myself, imposing strong moral judgments, fearing that my daughter will laugh at me. I feel like one of those tiny puppet dictatorships under communism, having no real clout of my own. And yet, like any parent, I have more authority than I imagine, mainly because I am still taller than her (but not by much), and can user bigger words. I argue with my daughter, and she argues right back to me in ways I'd never have dared with my own parents. Her dress is too sheer, or too tight, or too short. "You can't tell me what to do," she says.

But maybe I still can, because sometimes, more often than I would have imagined, she goes into her room and emerges five minutes later, wearing something even I like.

We are both vulnerable, both needy, both wanting to give the other room; just like any "normal" family with a girl in her teens. But no matter how "normal" domestic life sometimes seems, these years have tied the two us together with a knot incapable of being undone.

Samantha has become my friend, in big ways. She

watches the household food budget. When we go shopping for clothes, she looks for the T-shirts on sale. Sometimes, she'll even set or clear the table, without my asking.

"How was your day," she asks, when I come home pooped with exhaustion. My daughter sides with me against those who would harm me. If I let myself go completely, going into a riff about the trials and shortfalls of work, she'll rail against my co-workers, launching a vendetta against those who dare to come up against me. She takes my side against the world.

But now, I recall, I was my mom's protector, too. By my teens, I was my mother's confidante. I'd sit at the dinner table, listening intently, with mounting horror, while Mom told Dad about her job and the way, once again, they'd taken advantage of her. Then, when my father would shrug his shoulders, from out of the blue I'd declare myself on my mother's side. I'd urging her to carry on, insist that her boss give her a much-deserved raise. "Stand up for yourself!" I told my mother. "Really?" she said. "You think I can get it?" And she never once laughed at me.

This sense of my daughter as my protector is one of the great joys of my life. She, as much as anyone alive, knows my goals, understands my purpose. "You like to eat?" I asked her, when she complained I worked too hard. That settled her for all time.

Is this unhealthy, this sense of ingrown mutuality? I think not. I have seen children in large families learn naturally to protect each other. The oldest watches out for the youngest, and the youngest admires to the point of godhead her older brother. We have only each other, but the caring is just as great.

This search for someone to care for is part of the human family, it is inherent in our spirit. If Samantha did not want to shield me, looking out for how I've been scammed by the auto mechanic, how I've been wounded by colleagues or friends, I'd worry about her as a sociopath. So she loves her mom. Rather than become my mother, she is becoming my equal.

But not quite yet. For now, I am mostly Eema, a sign that she's got one foot out the door. Except when a squirrel gets into the house or a spider web is found on her wall. Then it's "Mommmmmy" and I run into her room, fooled by the imitation of real disaster. And I'm glad to be called at all.

August, 1996

Table for Three

Just around the time it seemed as if J was to be a fixture in her life, my daughter Samantha asked me, "Do you think I can call him Dad?"

"I think you should call him J," I said. Only lately, she had rudely called him "He," or "Him," and told me I could never love anyone else ever again. I thought "Dad" was something of a stretch.

Still, I can't deny my heart made a little leap. Dad. The word sounded at once natural and strange coming from her, a primeval echo of a world eternal yet suddenly new, one we'd left long ago.

In the first years after her father died, Samantha had longed for a Dad with an electric intensity that could light a small city. When we ate at the California Pizza Kitchen, she would interview the cutest waiter, asking, "Are you single? Will you marry my Mom?"

I was busy doing all the Dad-like things, convincing myself that by teaching my daughter to ride a bike, to fly a kite, to fish and toss a softball, she'd never know what she was missing. I was precisely the opposite of Mary Gordon's mother as portrayed in her autobiography, "The Shadow Man." Gordon's father (a liar, pornographer and anti-Semitic Jewish convert to Christianity, but that's another story) died when she was age 7, and the next day her mother packed up the house, tossed out Mary's toys and her father's belongings and moved the two of them in with Mary's grandmother.

She stopped working and never did a thing for herself again. I was, by contrast, a study in parental mitosis.

Lacking a husband with whom to share obligations, I split myself in two and then split again. I worked myself into a fury maintaining a home, changing light bulbs, attending swim meets, ball games and concerts ceaselessly anticipating the needs of my child. Each father's day I felt a comic rage that no one thought to buy me a tie!

But at hotel swimming pools while on vacation, Samantha would harness herself to other families and get the other fathers to launch her from their shoulders into the water. My sleight of hand had fooled only me.

Her yearning upset me deeply and I took pains to talk her out of it.

"What do you need a Dad for?" I asked her when she was six. She was heavily into dolls at the time, and her fantasies were that a Prince would come and whisk her away. "Go ahead, name one thing."

I thought of fathering as a series of tasks which could be performed by anyone, male or female. I made a list — earn a living, give stern punishments for minor failings, learn to use a soldering iron — and once I'd checked them off, I was done.

But Samantha was not content. To her, a toolbox did not make me a man, even if I did have a good set of wrenches. My daughter is an instinctive Freudian, a believer in the loaded notion that men are different than women at some essential level and can never be interchanged. Maybe it's the voice. Or the girth. Whatever the missing factor, when it came to filling the position of Dad, we had two different job descriptions in mind.

My desires were practical and open-ended, falling into the categories of General Contractor or Assistant Mom, able to fill any gaps I might have overlooked.

But Samantha's hopes have a broader, more operatic sweep. She thought of Ibsen's *Master Builder*, a carpenter who could recreate our family.

The death of her father had created an enormous

physical void, but it had created other injustices it took me ages to see. On her shoulders lay the extraordinary concern for me, my health and happiness. She checked up on me — Where am I? Why am I late? Who am I with? Did I get my annual physical exam? She could not bear to see me cry, lest my heart literally break.

She made judgments about my friends; the men I dated were evaluated and quickly deemed inadequate, as if she was the older and I the younger.

"What a drip!" she would say. "Can't you do better?" Our fates were linked: a father for her was a mate for me.

In time, we stopped going to places where Dads were required, and became a couple, the two of us. On my birthday one year in Oregon, she left the table and secretly ordered a special cake. She was a 10-year-old girl lugging her own baggage, making her own arrangements, keeping her own counsel. She learned to read maps, to talk politics, to bill food to a room, to do the weekly shopping. She could accompany me anywhere. Tough and brave, or merely tough. She had become her own Dad.

She was hungry, but never desperate. Samantha could see that there was something wrong with the pool of candidates for the office of Father. Her face was set in a continual frown of disbelief suggesting, "Is that all there is?"

"He'll have to be someone who loves both of us," I told her, but I couldn't imagine who that would be.

In the years alone, I have changed beyond recognition. Sturdy self-confidence emanated from every pore. I looked in the mirror trying to see myself through male eyes. J, who knew me back then, says I gave off absolutely no vibes. That isn't precisely true. I gave off the vibes of androgyny, the inter sexuality of a totally self-contained being. I was a woman striving for balance by incorporating the strengths and talents of a man. In this period I did my own rewiring of lamps after rejecting an affair with an electrician.

And then one day, long after Samantha gave up hoping, a light went on. Out of the shadows, a real man appeared.

It was not immediate. She still worships, of course, at the shrine of the One True Dad. But surely, I can see the current of Dadness moving between them. Last weekend, they sat at the dining room table conspiring over a math problem. They were cramming for her finals. Hour after hour he sat with her, going over the word problems, fractions and equations that seemed totally beyond her ken.

"I can't! I can't," she said, pleading with him.

"You can," he said.

And everything that I told her we'd been waiting for seemed to come true.

June, 1996

Weights and Measures

When my father was a boy, he was so thin that he qualified for the school nutrition breakfast every morning, which he supplemented with daily milkshakes.

This is the part of his childhood I've long known about, having been told the story often when I was growing up scrawny myself. But some things about his youth I didn't find out until this weekend, in the aftermath of his triple bypass surgery, like the novel weightlifting program he had designed while a young man.

"I used to go up to the roof of the apartment building," he told me. "And I'd take a brick and tie some heavy rope around it. Lifting the brick by its rope, that's the way I built up muscle."

And he kept it up, too. All these years later, I am astounded by how little I've known about my Dad, notably his discipline and focus. The way he sets his feet on a path and never loses his way. Just two weeks ago, though suspecting the shooting pain from his heart to his arm was angina, he was still effortlessly lifting suitcases in and out of the car.

It never did make sense, now that I think about it. The way he went from the reed-like man of his wedding photos to the bulky George C. Scott look-alike that I remember as a tower of strength from my teenage years. Somehow I attributed his bulking up to the rigors of married life and having to make a living for his family in hard times. His athletics, so far as I knew it, was limited to bowling.

But I didn't know, or wasn't paying attention. All those

years of wood and metal sculpting, building furniture, all of his hobbies are physical.

And last week it showed. For there he was, on the hospital bed at North Ridge Medical Center in Fort Lauderdale, only thirty hours after his sternum was cut and his arteries replaced with veins from his leg, he is the physical equal of Jack Palance doing one-arm pushups during the Academy Awards a few years ago.

The nurses came running to see the miracle of a man who will turn seventy-five this September, heaving himself all over the bed on his forearms, strong despite the pain. His feat is more than physical endurance. The more intense his physical agony, the more considerate he becomes of his nurses, his wife and children. An inner quiet pervades. Even in the face of disorienting amnesia, he is at one with his will.

In the days prior to my father's angiogram, I ask the rabbi for a prayer, a *me'shaberach* for his health and speedy recovery.

"What's your father's name?" "*Jacov ben Malka v'Shmuel.*" I think I'm being smart-assed, putting my father's mother's name first, but I'm brought up short.

"*Jacov ben Malka,*" he says, "that's how he's known."

This is interesting. According to tradition, whea Jew is allowed to approach the sacred Torah scrolls, it's typically our father's name that establishes our lineage. But when a man or woman is in critical danger, it's our mother who calls to us.

Why is this? Perhaps the tradition is teaching us to distinguish between the "outer" world and the "inner." There is a public realm — the name that the community knows us by — and there is the ultimate spiritual realm, closest to the womb, where we know our truest selves.

So maybe a person is like an onion, with layers of identity, waiting to be revealed.

There were 13 messages on my parents' answering

machine last Saturday. All news travels fast in the Bridgeview coop off Lake Ida Road in Delray Beach, Florida but none faster than the bad. Up and down Poppy Place and Privet Lane friends and neighbors are calling, the anxiety rising so high that one neighbor, Dave, comes over as soon as he sees our car parked in front of the condo.

My parents moved to Delray Beach about ten years ago, and at the time I thought they were nuts. All those old people! Why not move out to California, stay chronologically diversified, be closer to Samantha and me? But I was wrong. Family is important, but friendship has its glory too.

Mynn and Ruby live right down the street.

"Look, I made Jack a get well card!" says Ruby. He's a graphic artist with a fondness for acrylic posters exhorting against the problems of the inner city. And Mynn's a photographer. Ruby's 18 x 24 inch card says simply "Jack of all trades," with line drawings of hammers, pliers and other of my father's favorite tools.

Two years ago, Mynn had bypass surgery at North Ridge hospital with the very same surgeon who operated on my Dad. Mynn's health gives my parents confidence in their own.

"That Dr. Catinella. What a good looking man!" says Mynn happily. Then she looks at my mother and whispers, "I couldn't sleep Thursday night. I was so worried for you."

My mother's memory is selective.

"But Mynn, you never felt any pain did you?"

"Ha!" says Mynn. Once my mother used to worry about the values of my friends. Now the roles are reversed. I look at my parents' companions and I am relieved. They have good hearts and a talent for loyalty. I begin to wonder: How many people do I know who will worry for me?

"Look what we've put you two through," my mother moans to my brother and me, looking back on the terrors of the past year. She's just healing now from her own valve replacement surgery ten months ago.

I am startled by my lack of resentment. Loss is inevitable. In my prayers, I am trying to hold back the on-coming dark. So an aging parent is a gift, considering the alternatives. It feels good to visit my father, a privilege to reach him, even by phone. "What I'm really looking forward to," says my father via long-distance, "is using the weights at the gym." By more than muscle do we take the measure of the man.

June, 1996

All in the Family

By the time I got to Liberties Book Store in Boca Raton, Florida, last stop on a national tour for Jewish Book Month, I had my thirty-five minute stump speech down pat.

I was promoting an anthology about growing up Jewish and female in America and, even after sixteen cities and more than forty speeches, I still warmed to the task. I start with a very funny story about a big white pushka, that is, a charity box that is confused with a tampax container, then go on to new images of young girls hiding in the Ark alongside the Torah scrolls, then move into a poem of Grandma who had a lover. I love presenting my stories to new audiences, however much it occasionally makes me feel like Carol Channing in the one thousandth performance of *Hello Dolly*

But even after all those cities, Boca was to be different for many reasons, mostly because my parents live in nearby Delray Beach. My mother had a serious case of kvelling; I could hear her swell with pride months before I actually arrived. Having tried over many years to give them nachas now I was about succeed. My father had determined he would endure each of my four speeches, even when he would be the only man in a room of three hundred women and no matter how tedious the repetition might seem. The burden on me was great.

I arrived at the very bookstore where Dan Quayle had signed his own book on family values a few months ago, to find the rows of chairs filled with white-haired men and women. I recognized no one. No one smiled at me. It was almost 7:30. I was ready to begin.

As soon as I opened my mouth I knew something was wrong. I started with a joke about the eighty degree weather and how my parents, who were sitting in the back row, had told me to bring wool because Florida was cold. Not a smile in the room. I commenced the body of the speech, referring to my experience at Hebrew school in New York and my aunt Rita in Brooklyn, certifiable laugh-getters under normal conditions. Not a titter.

"I'm going to read 'The Big White Pushka,'" I announced, "and if you don't laugh, I'm going to be very worried about you." I read it. Karen Golden's story is hilarious, believe me. In the Everglades region of Davie the night before I had sold out on the strength of it. But in the Boca Raton book store off Mizener Park, I was laying a bomb.

Now I was seriously concerned. What would Henny Youngman do? I looked at my book jacket to see if I was reading from the wrong text. No, the book had my name on it. I went on with my program, cutting past all the one-liners straight to the information. Marjorie Morningstar. Philip Roth. Glazed looks came back at me. As I was reading, a dreadful thought occurred. Maybe I was there on the wrong night. Perhaps Liberties had actually scheduled a Cancer Care expert and everyone in my audience had been diagnosed with lymphoma!

With me that night was one of my contributors, a woman from Longboat Key, Florida named Shirley Fein. Mrs. Fein had never been published before and her appearance in my anthology alongside established and up-and-coming writers on the Jewish experience, was clearly a high point of her life. I introduced Shirley Fein, and the crowd immediately engaged with her. They laughed at a mention of her growing up in a farm in Connecticut and Grandpa, who had drawn dead bodies to the graveside as head of the Bialystock Chevra Kadisha. It ordinarily is not a laugh-getter, but it was reassuring to see that the people out front were breathing.

"What's going on?" I asked Arnold Fein, Shirley's husband, while she was reading her story.

"They're retired people," he told me. "They're not used to linear thinking."

But Arnold Fein was retired himself; his explanation just didn't feel right. They liked Shirley so well that I let her go on to talk about her difficulties being a left-handed girl growing up on a farm with a grandfather who wore Cossack boots and acted like the Tsar. Then I returned to the podium to close up the evening, reading another sweet reminiscence about Hebrew school, and opening it up for questions. One red-haired woman rose to say that her daughter had a wonderful adult bat mitzvah. I restrained an impulse to kiss her. But from the others, nothing.

"What's the matter?" I asked Sindy, the public relations advisor at Liberties.

"I don't know," she said. "I've never seen them so quiet. They always ask something."

"Well, thanks for coming," I announced, my shirt dripping with sweat. "Maybe you'll talk to me when I sign your book."I sat down, despair oozing out of every pore. I had been a failure, and my parents were there to witness it. What had gone wrong?

But just as I dug into my purse preparing for whoever might want my signature on the pages of my poor work, a crowd descended on me.

"Marlene! Do you remember me?" A horde of men and women were advancing toward the podium, books in hand, their faces beaming. The wax museum was coming to life! There was Bob and Annette from Westbury, Long Island. And Mynn and Ruby from Bridgeview, Florida. It was a scene from out of my brother's bar mitzvah 30 years before, only with more gray.

"Do you know me, Marlene?" asked Bernie. "I was the first one to diaper you."

His wife Evelyn told the story to the waiting throng. "Your father and mother invited us over and you needed to be changed. Your mother was busy, and your father was too nervous. And...

"And I," interjected Bernie, "was the expert on diapering since my daughter Robin was two months old at the time. I was the first male to see your bottom. That is, other than your Dad."

So it had been the roar of the past that drowned out their hearing. No wonder they couldn't laugh at my presentation. My mother and father rushed over to hug me. So happy, so loving, so neat and content. The joyful sound of kvelling filled the room. My mother took Bernie's hand. "Did he tell you he was the first to diaper you?" she asked.

"Bernie," I said in vast relief. "If I could have picked anyone, I'm so glad it was you."

November, 1996

Quality Time

The high school semi-formal was held last weekend and my daughter, Samantha, tried her best to be blasé.

She held off considering what dress to wear until the afternoon of the big event; only then, already costumed head to toe in black, did she concede that white patent leather shoes just wouldn't make it. With an hour to go before the dance began, we dashed to Nordstrom, where she tried on black high heels. Across the aisle, another mom looked on, laughing gently at our dilemma, while her own teenager weighed the relative merits of red or purple loafers in suede.

"These are me," Samantha said assertively as I purchased a pair of open toed sling backs. Her heels clicked on the parquet as we rushed out the door.

While my daughter was acting cool, I was having an anxiety attack. I remember high school dances only too well — impossibly stiff prom dress and bouffant hair making me look like Sandra Dee, fiddling aimlessly with the bowl of Cheetos at the dinner table, getting the orange cheese dust on my clothes and under my manicured fingertips while the band endlessly played "Donna;" the boys who used to crack me up so easily while dissecting a frog in biology class now standing tongue-tied and idly flapping their ties. "If you get cold feet you don't have to go," I told her even as I fork over the check paying for the dance ticket. I remembered surviving my dances by making small talk with the band, especially Frankie, the tall greasy-haired saxophonist, imagining myself in a white strapless dress in the gal-singer role of Doris Day. By evening's end, despair rising, I was home eating a whole box of Mallomars.

"You think you'll sing tonight?" I asked her.

"Oh, right!" she snarled.

I am such a loser, holding up my thumbs and forefingers in a big double L as Cher did in "Clueless." I am so 60s, so lost in my own generation's obsession with rules and propriety.

"You want me to look like a nun!" she cries, when I veto her mini skirt. Sure we listen to the same classic rock, mother and daughter tripping happily over the Shirelles and the Ronettes on the car radio. But we hear the lyrics from the opposite ends of time's megaphone. Samantha sees straight through her mom, the self-described one-time revolutionary. Anyone who knows all the words to "Will You Still Love Me Tomorrow?" is no feminist, see?

While she was preparing for the dance, pulling her hair back into a tight knot, then letting it go loose to her shoulders, then back into a knot, we fell silent, lost in reverie. I was recalling a similar hair obsession. Two years ago this week at her bat mitzvah, Samantha wore hair up in a French twist, looking so mature as she stood by the bimah that it scared her, too. Once the ceremony was completed, she flung it down.

Curiously, she was thinking of her bat mitzvah too. "Best day of my life," she said.

Am I exaggerating the influence of a single day in a girl's life?

"What this experience will teach you," the cantor had told her, "is how to master yourself." During the dress rehearsal, she stared blankly at the Torah scroll, her face blank with terror. But the next day, revived by her family and friends and beaming self-confidence, there was mastery. She had discovered what psychologist Mary

Pipher calls her "true self."

"Girls who hold on to their true selves are more likely to keep their relationship with their families alive," Pipher writes in the best-selling study of adolescent girls, "Reviving Ophelia." "Although they distance some, they do not totally abandon their families." Oh, if it should only be.

She is almost 15, tall, with a long stately neck and a lovely self-confident aura about her. She looks grown up to you, but to me.... well, she is still, as my mother says, my child. "Let's go out for coffee," my child says. "Let's have some quality time."

And I yearn for this quality time too. Quality time to hold her close, like when she was young, and tell her true stories about what the world has in store. Quality time to give her whatever protection my paltry moral lessons can afford. Quality time before the chaos of the world gets the upper hand.

"Things are gonna change so fast," sings Tori Amos in the teen anthem, "Winter," which is about the lost love of a girl for her father. "tell you that I'll always want you near/say that things change, my dear."

Things change, indeed, and she is not the only one to feel the wind at her back. There is a common theme, a common anxiety, among the high school parents I know. It is: Time Is Running Out. Any day now, our children will be gone.

For the first time in years, we men and women are talking to each other less about careers, and more about our kids.

"You can't talk to me until Finals Week is over," my friend Gloria said. Among ourselves parents are discussing the Middle Ages, graphing equations, the literary values of Medea and Oedipus.

There is an epidemic of concern, and of interest.

"I've made up my mind that these are the years that matter," my friend Brenda says. "I am going to be around more, even if it means driving carpool."

When Samantha was a baby, I used to marvel at my friends whose children were teenagers: how did they let them go?

"Oh, you'll be ready for it by then," they said. But I'm not ready now. My car is parked early in the hotel driveway waiting for the dance to end. I see her from a distance and a huge lump swelled in my throat. "Best dance ever," she said.

Say things change, my dear.

January, 1997

A Worrier's Delight

My Passover seder was acclaimed by one and all as, once again, the best ever. Good thing, too, since up to the last moment, anxiety dogged my every step.

First, I worried about the table setting, for this was my first seder al fresco, served not only outside but on plastic.

"I'm sure everyone will understand," said my mother. But I was not so sure. Fearing that my friends would think I was cheap or lazy, not nearly the Martha Stewart I pretend to be, I left frantic messages of warning: this seder would be "casual;" be sure to bring sweaters, and dress for the chill.

Then I worried about the food. Willie gave me three kosher chickens; Audrey was bringing two briskets. But what if still it wasn't enough?

"You're worried for nothing," my mother said. But by now, she was worrying too; not about my seder in Los Angeles, but my cousin Lorraine's in New York to which she was bringing a platter of fruit. We spent hours debating the relative merits of pineapples, strawberries, cantaloupe or a mix of all three and grapes. A worrier's delight.

With my mother thus preoccupied, I turned to cousin Rita. She was busy fretting about her table settings for her second night seder, and hadn't caught up to concern about the food. Thus, I went on alone. Beyond the natural concern my guests would die of starvation, I agitated about one cousin who eats only kosher, and another who eats only vegetables, those friends who are allergic or who are on the Zone diet or the protein diet or on Phen-Fen. I felt the kind of apprehension that made me long for Yom Kippur when no one eats at all. And when my worries had boiled and condensed into a fine fume, I baked a turkey breast and, for good measure, a potato kugel (doubling the recipe) and an extra dessert, an orange cake.

Little did I know that, in the midst of my obsession, my friends were worrying too. On Sunday, Leslie called, tormented about the shape of the hard-boiled eggs she had been requested to bring.

"Why did you give me something so easy to do?" she asked in exasperation. "I'm only good at hard tasks. I couldn't peel the eggs without leaving half the white in the shell. I threw out a bunch and those that I kept are so deformed, they're practically abstract.

"Finally it was 6 P.M. Monday. Willie, whose matzoh balls are internationally celebrated for flotation, came through the door frothing about her soup.

"Tasteless," she declared it, and the matzoh balls, she insisted, were like lead. So she salted the pot, added water to it, and nursed it like a baby, worrying all the way that she had paid too much for the chickens, and vowing that next year she would buy them closer to *yuntif*, when the kosher market sells them at half price.

Audrey and Tom arrived, their brisket kept warm in a huge professional corrugated box. Audrey declared the meat stringy and her sauce "too intense." By turns she threw herself into apoplexy, worrying that the meat would be either too hot or too cool and why can't she turn my stove top to "On."

Meanwhile, Karen came in disturbed to find that the chicken would be served unheated: "It's fine with me," she said with a glare of disapproval so firm I threw the chicken into the microwave, returning only to see her and Judy eye each others' carrots with suspicion. Whose would be best?

Then Marika sauntered in, warning one and all that her chocolate cake "is much better than it looks." Diane, not to be out-mortified, suffered the indignity of contributing only bottled grape juice.

"I can cook, too, you know," she said.

And with that, the seder itself began.

You'd think that my worries would end there and then but you underestimate my talent for a good hard-boiled distress. This year, as seder leader, I kept my worries about the haggadah to a minimum, refusing to rewrite it completely, making due with the one I had first compiled when all my guests were feminists. That left me only to bother about whether anyone would miss the washing of the hands ceremony (no one did), and to wonder why we never get beyond the first verse of *Chad Gad Ya*.

But Michael, who co-leads the seder each year had been worrying for me. Concerned that the seder would go over the heads of the children, he brought with him *Uncle Eli's Haggadah* off the Internet. Every ritual, every historic reference had its own Dr. Seuss-like rhyme.

"I think the seder is for children," he said, his voice filled with obligation.

What are these worries about? My mother says there are "good problems" and "bad problems," and these about Passover are of the first, happier, variety. How wonderful it is to worry about such small things. The weather, the table, the food and the guests. These are the concerns, the privileges of love.

Bad problems, of course, we know all too well. Heart conditions, unemployment, death. To know only good worries is to be in a state of bliss, to be part of a natural order in which most problems are resolved by time, and to learn once again that God is in the details.

Monday evening was the hottest night of the year. We sat on the patio, telling the story of the Exodus to freedom by the light of the full moon. Warmed by gentle breezes, we ate eggs (deemed perfect), soup (thick and flavorful), brisket (masterful), carrots (divine) and the world's greatest Passover chocolate cake. The children understood it all. "The best Passover ever!" they all declared. And boy was I glad I served on plastic.

April, 1997

We're Talking Chopped Liver

We arrived in New York at midnight and by 1 A.M. my mother was serving us dinner.

"It's too late, Mom," I say. "I'll just have some fruit."

A huge bowl of cut up pineapple, strawberries and melon was already on the table set for four, but that would not suffice. In our family there's a ritual: no visit officially begins unless we sit down together to eat a full meal.

Samantha and her grandmother had planned the dinner menu last week: Chicken soup with matzoh balls, followed by chopped liver. They agreed this was the perfect snack.

"You want the chicken soup?" my mother asks me. Samantha is already happily eating. My stomach is ready for bed. Then I spy the chopped liver, heaped into its crystal bowl. The pale brown color gave it away.

"You cooked!" I exclaim. My mother beams in delight. "You said you didn't cook any more."

My mother had valve replacement surgery last year, and recuperation has been slow. She gracefully accepted her limitations, substituting good take-out for the recipes she had spent a lifetime perfecting. But obviously, lethargy irked her: as soon as she felt better, she flew back to the kitchen as others bee-line to the gym or the golf course.

Looking at the liver, my heart makes a little leap. Hers really is the best in the world — sweet and pungent, with more flavor and grit than pate — but that is not the point. Worry about my mother has worn a groove in my shoulders, like my daughter's backpack.

Every phone call, every heavy silence, weighs me down. Even when I am not with her, I feel myself looking straight into her eyes; the burden grows.

But now: health has returned. Here, in a cut-glass tureen on the dining room table, is proof. From out of the depths of my traveler's exhaustion, hunger arises, not only in anticipation of what I might eat, but by the load that is lifting, my heart taking flight.

I have not eaten chopped liver in years. My friend Karen serves it at big gatherings of friends, but I'll take a polite nibble and then go on to carrot sticks and Perrier. In a world of the politically incorrect diet, chicken liver is worst of forbidden fare. A cardiologist's full employment act, chopped liver is high in cholesterol from both the meat and the eggs. But when my mother feels well enough to make chopped liver ..... the surgeon general be damned.

Some foods are not truly about eating. They are about higher forms of nourishment. History. Tradition. Family. Memory. Love. Junior's deli in Westwood sells 30 pounds of chopped liver (theirs is beef) a day. There are lot of "malnourished" people out there. When I was a child, my mother and I made chopped liver together whenever my parents entertained. It was part of my apprenticeship, an act of transformation (a girl becomes a woman, ugly foods become divine) that took the whole day. So, more than appetite, it is memory she is serving — both hers and mine — when she makes chopped liver today.

To make chopped liver for a small crowd, my mother sautés two sliced onions virtually all morning, so that the house fills with the sweet smell of vegetable sweat. She hard-boils four eggs, then places them in a glass bowl to cool in cold water. Then she adds half a pound of chicken livers to the onion and cooks them until the pink is gone and they've turned a lifeless gray. (When I was in high school biology, I thought nothing of dissecting a frog. After all, I had already cooked raw chicken liver — hideous, slimy, and untouchable in its blood. Nothing could phase me.)

Now we are ready to grind. Before the days of the food processor (use the "pulse" function, it gets the same result) my mother had one of those heavy cast-iron grinders that clamped onto the side of the table, and demands the upper body strength of the Nordic track. The grinder looked like a small tuba, with a wide mouth at the top, and a cylindrical tube and a wooden handle which pulverized the food into quarter-inch round streams.

If I hated touching the liver, I was fascinated by the grinding, a sensual experience worthy of Freud. First the onions and the eggs are pushed together down the feed tube, followed by the cooked liver; my fingers breaking, probing and squishing the whites and the yolks, the skins of the caramelized onion wrapping around my wrist, the innards of the liver climbing over my hands. I feel the exaltation of hard work: Leaning my body into the grinder, I lift and pull the grinder handle, round and round. Out they come, strands of yellow, gold and reddish brown coils of egg, onion and meat, which, when mixed with salt and pepper and spread on rye bread, as the poet George Herbert said, "makes drudgery divine." When I told my mother I would be writing about her chopped liver this week, she first reddened at the compliment, then blanched.

What would people think of her, still making food as dangerous and suspect as carrying a concealed weapon?

"They won't want it," she said.

Surely there is a way to capture the legacy that comes with making chopped liver — the grind and the grandeur — without invoking its 90 megaton cholesterol wallop. Back in Los Angeles, I began a frantic search for an answer. Four recipes later, I presented my mother with my friend Rona's recipe for "mock chopped liver" (courtesy of Aunt Rose of Delray Beach, Fla.) as what we'd both been waiting for.

Mom knew Aunt Rose's recipe all along.

"It's not for me," she declared. "I like the real thing."

To each her own.

May, 1997

Mock Chopped Liver

Caramelize 3 onions in one tablespoon oil; add one 15 ounce can LeSueur petite peas; 1 cup walnuts, finely chopped; eight egg whites (hard-boiled) and two yolks (hard-boiled). Place ingredients in food processor. Pulse (about 10 times for each addition). Mix in a bowl.

Salt and pepper to taste. Refrigerate.

Family Man

The restaurant billboard advertised its Father's Day brunch in letters too large to miss.

"If I had a father, we could take him out to eat," my daughter said, as we drove by.

Samantha's voice held no accusation; she was entirely matter of fact. But I took it personally anyway; her words signaled that my severed ties with J could hurt her as well.

I squirmed helplessly. I can squirrel and save for her hiking boots, singing lessons, the dress for the family party; I'd move the world for my girl. But there's nothing I can do about getting her a dad.

My friends get angry with me when I turn on myself.

"So what," says Nessa, her voice growing tight. "So you couldn't get her a dad. She had her own dad, and she'll remember him."

And Arlyne, newly single, gets practically frantic at my self-castigation.

"Listen," she says as we sip our lattes, "I can't stand it when a guy uses my children to get to me."

If that's what happened, I was a willing co-conspirator.

It is true and can be said without a trace of shame: No mother can resist a family man. I loved the man who loved my daughter. I couldn't help it.

I had relegated Father's Day to the ranks of unobserved customs, like Christmas or Chinese New Year, one that others might honor with full regalia but that we, in our family, spent at the movies or otherwise ignored.

And then came J. Whatever a dad could mean, he was

it. Last Father's Day, Samantha and I took J to the Getty Museum and then out to dinner. We each felt audacious, risky. J had never been a dad. Samantha hadn't had a dad in a long time. And, after so many years going solo, I no longer knew what a dad to my daughter might be.

"You're not my father, and you never will be!" Samantha screamed at him outside the Getty parking garage.

"You're right," J said. He didn't want to be her father, full of fearsome duty and overweening expectation. But being her dad — authoritative, respecting, care-giving in a benign sort of way — this was something he might be able to do well. He assisted with her homework, discussed her music, attended her concerts and singing lessons. He bought her a guitar. There was no "we" without her; wherever J and I went, Samantha was expressly invited to come.

"Don't you two want to spend more time alone?" she asked. "Don't you need some personal space, some private time together?"

If only we'd listened.

Our three-way connection seemed preordained, like a trinomial equation set into motion long ago; he was the kind of man I'd promised Samantha years before, one who could love us both.

At the Getty, J showed Samantha the red figures painted on black fragments of Greek urns, the remnants of a great civilization that had come and gone. At dinner, he let her taste his wine. I watched them from my side of the triangle and felt myself begin to breathe. We were a threesome; the number three, in Hebrew, is *gimel*, meaning full and ripe.

He was among the few "dads" to attend the high school parent meetings. He knew the dean, the music coach and her instructors by sight. He e-mailed the math teacher on her behalf, arguing that Samantha understood more algebra than her grades indicated. Sometimes, he spoke for me. Samantha judged her success by his approval and was crushed by his criticism. He was a dad in every way.

We were a family, but not a couple, and that's why we hung on so long.

Now comes the sad part. The end.

When love fades, is it God's error or our own? Or just a fact of life?

I give the three of us this much: We meant it for good. J loved being a dad. Samantha loved having a dad. He loved being part of "us." She loved having a larger "us." And, among everything else, I loved saying, "Table for three."

Even when things grew bad between J and me as man and woman, when our conversations became increasingly about Samantha and less about ourselves, as a dad, he kept at it. Up to the last minute, he judged her party dress for appropriateness, escorted her to family dinners, and gave her guidance on hiking gear; Samantha was still telling her friends about going to the movies with her "parents," taking great pleasure in an extra "s." She didn't lose faith.

"I only want what makes you happy," Samantha said.

"But J..." I started to say.

"I'll get over it," she said. "I'm stronger than you think."

But what about me?

June, 1997

A Perfect Orange

In addition to the usual bathing suits, socks and jeans shorts on the inventory list suggested by Camp Hess Kramer, Samantha received a separate letter announcing that the official colors for her Leadership 1997 sweat shirt this summer are orange and blue: orange for the body of the sweatshirt, blue (preferably royal) to spell out the words 'Leadership '97' on the front, and her name on the back.

Right away, I could forsee trouble.

Leadership is a very big deal at Wilshire Boulevard Temple camp which, after 45 years and 50,000 campers, is a very big part of Los Angeles Jewish life. For those 1,100 campers who will attend either Hess Kramer or its sister, Gindling Hilltop, this summer Leadership walks on hallowed ground. Coming a stage before CIT, two steps below *counselor*, Leadership is the crowning achievement of camper life; part in-crowd, part initiation into real authority.

"We sit with Administration!!!" as Samantha reminded me, nervously eyeing this marker of her impending adulthood. Or, as Howard Kaplan, camp director, wrote Samantha last February in his letter of congratulations: "You become the bearer of a tradition at Camp Hess Kramer, and you become a role model for hundreds of younger campers who look up to you." Mostly, it's a lot of fun, marked by a three day hike, lots of singing, cheering and in-jokes, and of course the distinguishing sweat shirt. It all adds up to what most Leadership alumni still recognize as "the time of their lives."

"It comes at exactly the right moment when they're most idealistic," Steve Breuer, executive director of Wilshire Boulevard Temple, told me. He created the Leadership program when he was camp director a generation ago. "But because campers expect it to be wonderful, it is."

As a parent, I say, it's wonderful for me, too. Jewish summer camp is a 20th Century American innovation and not enough can be said in its favor. Through camp life we see contemporary Judaism in its three eternal verities: One-part Zionism, one-part spiritual effusion, one part American pioneer spirit, campfire and all. Camp builds all three into our children, mixing toasted s'mores with the *hora*, and, if this is indoctrination, it works. I grew up thinking *If I Had a Hammer* was the Israeli kibbutz anthem. It didn't do me any harm.

Certainly if they could bottle camp, and the feelings of purpose and joy a happy camper brings into my family life, I'd be the first to buy. As for Leadership '97, my daughter has been looking forward to this special summer since her first 10-day session at Hess Kramer seven years ago. From the very beginning, camp has been the True North; its songs, its rituals, its celebration of Shabbat, its values provide the markers of real life, making much of what we do at home seem like filling time. In addition to locking in Jewish values, camp may provide the only positive social experience, and the only Jewish community, a child ever knows. Camp administrators would be more than great tour guides; they'd know how to make the Zionistic link explicit.

Which is to say that, if Howard Kaplan, and Craig Marantz, God's surrogate as Leadership Unit Leader, want orange and blue sweat shirts this summer, well, who are we to judge?

A week before camp's opening day we began the search. Let me tell you, sweat shirts come in 3,000 shades of gold, yellow, peach and red. Likewise, there are 12 brands of orange T-shirt — long sleeve, short sleeves, T-shirts with blue logos (Nike, Reebok, Ralph Lauren). We've gone from Oshman's to Macy's to Sportmart: In all Los Angeles, not one sweat shirt in *naranja*. We were dismayed but resolute. Having failed at finding the perfect orange sweatshirt, we would make one ourselves. What could there be to it?"

We'll dye a white one," I said, as if I coloring apparel is an every-day affair in my home. But after visiting a dozen stores, and finding dyes mostly in black and brown, I was turning pale.

"Do you think we can use food coloring?" I asked the check-out clerk at Vons. I described my plan to mix 12 drops of red with 24 drops of yellow. An elderly gentleman shook his head. "A sweatshirt is not a hard-boiled egg," he said.

So we kept searching store to store until, the day before she was to leave for camp, we came upon a bottle of RIT labeled "Tangerine" in a market close to home.

"That's it!" declared Samantha. "It's Tangerine," I said. "It will be orange enough for me."

We still had to acquire the letters, royal blue. The House of Fabrics had a white iron-on cut-out alphabet, or large pieces of blue iron-on felt; no pre-cut letters in blue. So we bought white letters and royal blue paint and stayed up all night coloring every single character of Leadership '97. In a wild, manic, way it turned out to be fun. I began to think that the Camp officials in their wisdom had not sent us on a wild goose chase after all. The sweat shirt was simply a form of karma yoga, forging spirit and responsibility in campers by purposely making them (and their parents) create the sweat shirts themselves.

Then the big day was upon us, and we packed the orange/tangerine sweat shirt, bathing suits and all into the car. I drove my daughter up to camp; Samantha ran to Craig Marantz like he was a long-lost cousin. I could only stand and stare.

"Your sweat shirt!" I said to Craig. "Why is your sweat shirt red?" Moreover, why was his lettering in white?

"Didn't anyone tell you?" he asked benignly. "The parents all complained, so they changed the color to red."

My face, in the car mirror, was a perfect orange.

August, 1997

Single Parent Cheers

I was late getting home from my meeting the other night. Too late to help my daughter prepare for her Spanish quiz. Too late to massage her shoulders after baseball practice. "Do Not Disturb," read the sign on her door. Her nightstand light was on, but Samantha was already asleep.

Disregarding her warning sign, I entered, and pulled the covers over her.

"Sweet dreams," I whispered, and kissed her forehead. Her body eased and relaxed. I knew from our car-phone talk that she'd had a good day. Still, until I saw Samantha myself, her body dressed for sleep in sweats, her hair neatly pulled back with a barrette, I could not rest. At nearly 16, my daughter is accustomed to making her own meals, putting herself to bed. The balance of power has shifted: I need the good night kiss more than she does.

I've been a single parent a long time now. I know a lot about it. When Jewish organizations need a speaker about single parenting, they often ask me. According to the Council on Jewish Federations, 12.5 percent of all Jewish children are being raised by single parents — 132,000 children nation-wide. But the number may even be higher. In Los Angeles, according to the new Los Angeles Jewish community population survey, 15 percent of all households with children under 18 are raised by single parents; nearly one in six. Jews may have fewer teen pregnancies than the surrounding American community, but we have lots of divorce, lots of widowhood, lots of single parents by choice. And the questions I'm asked most often are: how do you do it?

How do you make choices about the child's welfare without someone to bat the ideas around with? How do you play good-cop/bad cop by yourself? How do you get any time for yourself after a long day's work when a crying child is afraid to go to sleep? How do you retain a social life that doesn't leave the child feeling excluded?

The answers change with time. Raising a child is so overwhelming. "There's no school for parenting," my mother used to tell me, and single parents are even more in the dark. Tears to hugs, fears to snarls, zero to sixty. Whipped about in the heady winds of a child's emotions, with no other parent to provide an anchor. Yet, somehow, homework gets done, new Adidas get bought. We get through the school semester. We get over our tantrums. We get hugs. I get by, with a little help from my friends.

I'm not kidding. Some nights I can't bear the weight of the worry. And some days I have to *kvell* out loud. In either case, I talk: to the pillow, or to Marika, Jane or Willie. Or to God. I hold back nothing back. My advice to single parents: pick your friends wisely. Forget the meaning of shame. And learn the meaning of "pride."

It's about pride that I want to make a special point. A single parent's life is generally deemed to be one of pity, sadness, handicap. The prevailing attitude of our synagogues and organizations, and of married couples who belong to them, is that we are "broken," while they, of course are "in tact." In a series of focus groups sponsored by Jewish Family Service in Los Angeles, single parents reported that they felt "unwelcome" in Jewish life. There's a bias toward the nuclear family; anyone who doesn't conform is a challenge and a threat to community norms.

Perhaps it goes back to the Biblical commandment of caring for the widow and orphan, but single parents, in addition to extraordinary financial and emotional obligations, carry a weighty psychological burden to prove their wholeness. The Jewish single parent, because of our mythic indoctrination in Biblical stories about the nuclear family going back to Abraham and Sarah, is regarded as a war veteran, like the one-legged guy who stand on the highway with a tin cup. Battle scarred, needing help.

The aura of handicap which hangs over single families not only hurts parents, who ache with a sense of their own inadequacy, but it destroys the burgeoning confidence of our children.

Can it be that being a single parent is normal? Well, in my house it is. I didn't exactly plan to raise my child alone, but even so, it is a rewarding life. I love her, and she's still talking to me so I can't be doing too bad a job. I was lucky to do her bat mitzvah alone, without a spouse to argue with over "how Jewish" it would be. I have vacations with my daughter each year that are the envy of many two-parent families. We have closeness and intimacy.

I'm a single parent, sure. Glad of it.

February, 1998

Four Takes on Fifty

Take #1: Round Numbers

I was too young to turn 30; I was still a child, vacillating between independence and rebellion, even though I was already married and a property owner. At 30, I believed that love is all there is; that politics could be an extension of love and that psychotherapy was the pneumatic tool capable of tunneling through a closed heart. Foolish, of course, but also sweet. As I say, I was still so young.

Ten years later, I was too old to be merely turning 40. I had buried my husband, and watched my five year old daughter turn a shovel of dirt on her father's grave. I was older than everyone; older than my parents who, after all, still had each other; older than all my friends, who still played tennis and seemed to think that life was fun. I was older than the world, which is why I could only speak to God.

At 40, I believed that duty is all there is; that politics is an extension of obligation to others, and that ritual and spirituality are the escalator we ride when our feet are incapable of walking. Recalling this, I feel bitter, as if life did me a bad turn. As I say, I was already old.

Fifty, which I will turn next August, feels good. The number 50 seems full and round and open. Like my life. At almost 50, I'm tempted to quote the Zen master and say that the present is all there is. Or to quote the psychologist, that our history determines our fate. Neither is completely true. The present, unless enriched by history, can make us desperate for results. And history, unless sweetened by good work, community and friendship, can make us sad.

I believe now that I deserve to be happy. To me, politics is what happens when problems can't be solved by people on their own; that yes, psychotherapy can lead to insight, but only if there is enough will; that you don't have to scream in order for God to hear you, but it's not enough to talk to God, alone. Neither politics, psychotherapy or spirituality are a substitute for a good life.

Take #2: The Man/Woman See-Saw

Interestingly, my father established the optimistic tone by which I greet maturity. He never had the slightest word to say about 30 or 40, maybe because I was such a lost cause he couldn't reach me, or because he was such a young man himself, still engrossed in his own vision.

"A woman gets better as she gets older," my father said one day. "A man of 50, if he hasn't made it, he's finished. But a woman just begins to fly."

This of course, was my father's tribute to my mother, our own Amelia Earheart who has never lost her way. Mom waited many years to take flight. At 50, her career in insurance had begun to drag, and she went back to school. By 60, when Dad was exhausted from a working life, she finished college and became the financial wizard she was always meant to be. He turned inward, but she was raring to go.

The Man/Woman See-Saw — men go down just as women go up — has not be easy to accept. After Burton died, I said to myself, "no more older men," because why would I need them? Men find younger women attractive as a symbol of youth. Women seek older men as a symbol of strength. I wanted to meet a man on level ground.

Why hadn't my father told me then about life's ironies? Men get shaky in their 40s just as women get stable. Send in the clowns. The mid-life crisis is making mincemeat of most of the men I know. Meanwhile, the women get stronger by the day. One day, we will meet again, on our own vulnerable terms. I hope the meeting doesn't take next 10 years.

Take #3 Mother/Daughter Reunion

"Matrophobia," a word coined by Adrienne Rich, is the fear of becoming one's mother," and it is particularly relevant to women about my age, who hope to make peace and move on.

I have become a lot like my mother in recent years. Perhaps I was implanted with a time-release capsule making me interested in financial investments and the recipe for mandelbread. Were I not to be like her, who would I be? The self-made woman is great in her 30s, she is free of guilt, a tiger of talents and desires. But by 50, this self-made woman floats soul-less, belongs nowhere. My mother's finest qualities are magnificent, while her fierce independence, her physical strength and determination — those traits which I once dreaded — are becoming useful, are part of the comforts of home

Take #4 What makes a good life

When my husband was 50, I made him a lavish surprise party, including a gourmet dinner, a pianist, and guests in black tie. My friends and I, celebrating our own half-century, are off to Palm Springs soon, for a weekend at the spa.

How great we look, my friends and I. How luxurious the companionship feels. Once I looked at older women, and nearly cried. They weathered badly, or so it seemed to me. Now it doesn't matter much at all, and anyway, what can I do about it?

The important lessons about the good life seem to be these:

Keep ties with your old friends, especially those from

your school days; they know the meaning of fun.

Do good work, not for money or publicity, but for its own sake.

Expect no rewards; the harder you work, the luckier you get.

Share your wealth. Being cheap hurts your spirit, and doesn't postpone your death by a minute.

Love your family.

Maintain a sex life however old you get. Or keep the-dream of one.

August, 1998

Still Dead

My friend Jane and I met for dinner last week and had a good laugh about death. California's political campaign season is just commencing and we were discussing, in an off-hand way, what Burt, an attorney, might have made of an upcoming ballot proposition, were he still among us.

"It's amazing that he's still dead," I said, without quite knowing what I meant. Simultaneously, Jane and I let out a roar, a "yipes!" of astonishment, as people do when they touch something hot, or come too close to the *sitra atra*, what Kabbalists call "the other side."

"It's a bore isn't it?!" Jane said, rising to the occasion. "Still dead, after all this time."

Jane's father, Harold, is still dead, too. He died years ago of a painful illness. He was a large, strapping former football player who exuded robust physicality and wisdom; one of those men who add extra wattage to the earth's light.

"It's impossible that he's really gone," she said. "I want to say to my father, 'Enough already. I've learned to live without you. I'm not mourning anymore. It's safe for you to come back.'"

It's yet another yahrzeit, literally, "year-day" of memory, this one Number 11. And strangely, I, too, feel safe. The brutal purple blossoms of the jacaranda tree no longer assault my eyesight as they did years after the funeral. Our daughter, Samantha, has burst out of childhood and is almost ready to drive a car. The icicles of loss don't shiver down my grieving back any more.

And Burton himself is ancient history: He died before the advent of fax and modem (though he was the among the first to own a car phone), or self-stick postage stamps. We are living in two different worlds, he and I, the Before and the After. The dead don't grow or expand their horizons, you know.

But they do call to us, in their own time. And each May, at yarhzeit, death comes for a visit, bringing its own pots and pans to prepare its own food, much like my grandfather, who kept kosher, long ago. Death drinks its shnapps out of a yahrzeit glass and sits down at the table to talk for the twenty-four hours or so until the candle of memory is consumed. And I, like a character in a Kafka short story, wait on death and clear the crumbs of its wisdom off the tablecloth, trying to glean a message from this force beyond my control. As a temporary visitor, death has its charms, after all.

By an accident of the Jewish calendar, Burton's yahrzeit always falls around Mother's Day. The conjoining of the two by now seems right to me, though it is hardly the sappy vision of suburban complacency that the makers of Hallmark cards had in mind. Each year I try choose which to honor, birth or death. But inevitably the two come together, in the mixed bag that is life.

That last year on Mother's Day, Burt called our cousin Willie from the hospital and had her buy me a necklace of tourmaline hearts. I sat with him on his narrow bed, the hearts stared up threateningly at me. Two days later, Burton was gone, and my life as a single mother began.

But death has always been present at my family's Mother's Day. When I was a child, my mother spent the day in a kind of mournful haze recalling her own mother who had died when she was twelve. She felt cheated and there was nothing I could do to make up for it.

Death sat at our breakfast table where my brother and I served her home-made pancakes. She was appreciative, but distant. Dead, my mother was thinking. Still dead.

Eventually, and far too young, I learned about the perils of love and the cost of personal connection which is the true human dilemma. We spend a lifetime building a network of comfort and stability with parents, siblings, children, doomed to fervid mourning when they're gone. The reward for loving well is grieving well. The cost of weaving is in the tear. We live in the here and now, but the *sitra atra* is always close by.

As we studied last week's Torah portion, Tazria, the laws of childbirth, the rabbi asked for a show of hands: Who among us in the sanctuary had never suffered miscarriages, abortions, infertility? Who among the rest of us had not yet lost a parent or a sibling? We are all experienced in the litany of grief. We stand in the shadow of those who are still, still dead.

Our modern world, of course, is notoriously uncomfortable about death. Not for us the washing of the body, the sitting with the corpse, the acknowledgment that this end will be ours. All we've done is suppress the truth. It comes out obsessively, ridiculously, inopportunely. Why do we endlessly watch the funerals of Princess Diana and Mother Teresa? Why do we cry at the death of Paul McCartney's wife, Linda? It's easier to hurt for the grieving Beatle than to serve the memory of our own.

I prefer the Chassidic way, and the tales which give death the power and the majesty it is due.

Here, for example, is the 19th century story of Rabbi Loew who tried to subvert the Angel of Death. One day the Angel of Death came into Rabbi Loew's town near Yom Kippur. He carried with him a long scroll on which was inscribed the names of those synagogue members who were to die by plague in the coming year. The rabbi confronted the Angel of Death and ripped from his hands the scroll. He tore off the list, throwing the parchment into the fire. Every one was saved; but one name was left on the scroll, and it was his own.

I like this guy: He knew what the odds were. And he went out fighting.

May, 1998

Circle of Friends

When I was nine I had a fight with my best friend, Sharyn. Sharyn said something mean; I said something meaner, and soon we were down on the grass.

I pulled her hair. She pulled my hair. I can still feel the yank in my scalp where she went at me; and the way my own hands felt as I grabbed her long curly blond pony tail and tugged for all I was worth.

Afterwards, I was expected to feel ashamed of myself, but I never did. I felt cleansed of rage. Here was my best friend. If I couldn't get into it with her, than with whom? The battle felt honest, the struggle of two equals, and we got to the heart of the matter in the way words never could.

And that is how I know friendship, the high-stakes facing off of loyalties, fair and square.

A writer called the other day, asking me about my friendships for a book on women at mid-life. Her questionnaire read "Have any of your close friends died within the last few years?" Though my answer was "No, Thank God," I was startled enough to cry.

This is the one part of turning fifty that I haven't faced. I have accepted the end of child-bearing; the end of my daughter's babyhood; my parents' aging and the fact that I'll never again play the ingenue or sing bra-less with a rock 'n roll band (actually I was only part of the audience.) That things may happen to my *friends* is completely unacceptable.

Each of my friendships has been a test of wills, a firing of the glaze, a circumcision of the heart. Each friend has taken a piece from me, and given a piece back. When my friends go to the doctor these days, I want to know why.

I can remember like light through a diamond the stunning moment when each friendship took shape, the confrontation that shattered two wills trying to merge as one.

For Marika and me, it was a summer 30 years ago in Europe. We fought over what restaurant to eat in; what city to travel to; what friends to include in our evening's outings. We agreed on nothing, except that neither of us would walk away.

With Jane, it was a walk down Ventura Blvd, screaming to each other over our careers, and alternative visions of how to live a life.

With Susan, it was my fear that I had lost her when her babies were born.

With Cindy, it was my big mouth, going on about a guy she liked, now long gone.

Let's be frank, I'm not an easy friend. Signing on with me is hard labor. I pick fights, I imagine slights, I call in the middle of the night and worry that the end of the world is nigh. I have a lot of crises and need my hand held. Or else I withdraw completely, and you'll never know how I'm feeling even if you come after me with a cattle prod.

That's ok, because all my friends are like this too.

"If you lift the load, I will lift it too" it says in the Talmudic tractate Baba Kama, "but if you will not lift it, I will not either." Friendship is all about lifting. All my friends are heavy maintenance, all need constant attention. So be it. Good friendships to me are more valuable than good lovers, and harder to find.

But loyalty, understanding, patience and attentiveness — the four horseman of companionship — these are airborne like yeast, but much harder to brew than beer.

The difference for me between a casual friendship and a bosom buddy is whether we've ever had a serious fight. If I haven't argued with you over the years, it's just a matter of time.

A friend is someone who sits with you while you have your mammogram; or tells you to your face that your new diet is wacky; who waits to make sure you car starts in the parking lot even if you bought the car last month. When you're out of work, a friend calls everyone she knows until you have a job interview or lets you obsess endlessly about your business plan, like pie in the sky. When you've become a hermit, she calls to remind you that you've been working too hard and why haven't you been meeting any new men lately? And if you have no good answer, she'll ask all her friends until there's someone interesting for you to meet at least for lunch. A friend remembers to ask how your parents are, even if they haven't recently been ill.

A good friendship can never end.

When I was 30, I invited my four best friends to have lunch with me at the old Scandia restaurant up in Hollywood. I knew that they would love each other on sight.

Within seconds, we were back in the Queens playground. There was a conversation about shoes, I distinctly remember, and the relative value of high heels versus flats. Jane nearly took off her flat and threw it at Rena. But much as they disliked each other, when it was all over, they still liked me.

Yes, a good friendship is possible between men and women, but too often it is confused with marriage. Marriage is about time and space, the family to be built, and the home to be shared. But friendship is portable, fungible, enduring through all seasons.

As mighty as a storm. As sweet as a breeze.

July, 1998

About the Author

Marlene Adler Marks is an award-winning nationally syndicated columnist based in the *Jewish Journal of Greater Los Angeles,* where she was managing editor for more than a decade. She is a frequent contributor to newspapers and magazines including the *Los Angeles Times* and *Hadassah*. She is the editor of the anthology, *Nice Jewish Girls: Growing Up in America* (Plume/Penguin) and a popular speaker on women and political issues. She and her daughter, Samantha, live in Malibu, California.

Copies of A WOMAN'S VOICE: REFLECTIONS ON LOVE, DEATH, FAITH, FOOD & FAMILY LIFE, by Marlene Adler Marks, are available directly from the publisher at the address below.

A WOMAN'S VOICE is also available on the web through your favorite on-line bookseller or at our website.

ON THE WAY PRESS
23852 PACIFIC COAST HIGHWAY
SUITE 504
MALIBU, CALIFORNIA 90265
TEL: 310.456.1546. FAX: 310.456.7686

email: onwaypress@aol.com
http://members.aol.com/onwaypress